FACTS ON FILE
SCIENCE EXPERIMENTS

Physical Science Experiments

Pamela Walker
Elaine Wood

Facts On File
An imprint of Infobase Publishing

Physical Science Experiments

Text and artwork copyright © 2010 by Infobase Publishing

Editor: Frank K. Darmstadt
Copy Editor for A Good Thing, Inc.: Betsy Feist
Project Coordination: Aaron Richman
Art Director: Howard Petlack
Production: Victoria Kessler
Illustrations: Hadel Studios

Facts On File, Inc.
An imprint of Infobase Publishing
132 West 31st Street
New York NY 10001

Library of Congress Cataloging-in-Publication Data
Walker, Pam, 1958-
Physical science experiments / Pamela Walker, Elaine Wood.
p. cm.—(Facts on File science experiments)
Includes bibliographical references and index.
ISBN 978-0-8160-7807-3
1. Physical sciences–Experiments–Juvenile literature. 2. Physical sciences–Study and teaching (Middle school)–Activity programs. 3. Physical sciences–Study and teaching (Secondary)–Activity programs. I. Wood, Elaine, 1950- II. Title.
Wood, Elaine, 1950- . Title.
Q164.W23 2010
500.2078–dc22 2009023673

Facts On File books are available at special discounts when purchased in bulk quantities for businesses, associations, institutions, or sales promotions. Please call our Special Sales Department in New York at 212/967-8800 or 800/322-8755.

You can find Facts On File on the World Wide Web at http://www.factsonfile.com

Printed in the United States of America

IBT AGT 10 9 8 7 6 5 4 3 2 1

This book is printed on acid-free paper.

Contents

Preface

For centuries, humans have studied and explored the natural world around them. The ever-growing body of knowledge resulting from these efforts is science. Information gained through science is passed from one generation to the next through an array of educational programs. One of the primary goals of every science education program is to help young people develop critical-thinking and problem-solving skills that they can use throughout their lives.

Science education is unique in academics in that it not only conveys facts and skills; it also cultivates curiosity and creativity. For this reason, science is an active process that cannot be fully conveyed by passive teaching techniques. The question for educators has always been, "What is the best way to teach science?" There is no simple answer to this question, but studies in education provide useful insights.

Research indicates that students need to be actively involved in science, learning it through experience. Science students are encouraged to go far beyond the textbook and to ask questions, consider novel ideas, form their own predictions, develop experiments or procedures, collect information, record results, analyze findings, and use a variety of resources to expand knowledge. In other words, students cannot just hear science; they must also do science.

"Doing" science means performing experiments. In the science curriculum, experiments play a number of educational roles. In some cases, hands-on activities serve as hooks to engage students and introduce new topics. For example, a discrepant event used as an introductory experiment encourages questions and inspires students to seek the answers behind their findings. Classroom investigations can also help expand information that was previously introduced or cement new knowledge. According to neuroscience, experiments and other types of hands-on learning help transfer new learning from short-term into long-term memory.

Facts On File Science Experiments is a six-volume set of experiments that helps engage students and enable them to "do" science. The high-interest experiments in these books put students' minds into gear and give them opportunities to become involved, to think independently, and to build on their own base of science knowledge.

As a resource, *Facts On File Science Experiments* provides teachers with new and innovative classroom investigations that are presented in a clear, easy-to-understand style. The areas of study in the six-volume set include forensic science, environmental science, computer research, physical science, weather and climate, and space and astronomy. Experiments are supported by colorful figures and line illustrations that help hold students' attention and explain information. All of the experiments in these books use multiple science process skills such as observing, measuring, classifying, analyzing, and predicting. In addition, some of the experiments require students to practice inquiry science by setting up and carrying out their own open-ended experiments.

Each volume of the set contains 20 new experiments as well as extensive safety guidelines, glossary, correlation to the National Science Education Standards, scope and sequence, and an annotated list of Internet resources. An introduction that presents background information begins each investigation to provide an overview of the topic. Every experiment also includes relevant specific safety tips along with materials list, procedure, analysis questions, explanation of the experiment, connections to real life, and an annotated further reading section for extended research.

Pam Walker and Elaine Wood, the authors of *Facts On File Science Experiments*, are sensitive to the needs of both science teachers and students. The writing team has more than 40 years of combined science teaching experience. Both are actively involved in planning and improving science curricula in their home state, Georgia, where Pam was the 2007 Teacher of the Year. Walker and Wood are master teachers who hold specialist degrees in science and science education. They are the authors of dozens of books for middle and high school science teachers and students.

Facts On File Science Experiments, by Walker and Wood, facilitates science instruction by making it easy for teachers to incorporate experimentation. During experiments, students reap benefits that are not available in other types of instruction. One of these benefits is the opportunity to take advantage of the learning provided by social interactions. Experiments are usually carried out in small groups, enabling students to brainstorm and learn from each other. The validity of group work as an effective learning tool is supported by research in neuroscience, which shows that the brain is a social organ and that communication and collaboration are activities that naturally enhance learning.

Experimentation addresses many different types of learning, including lateral thinking, multiple intelligences, and constructivism. In lateral thinking, students solve problems using nontraditional methods. Long-established, rigid procedures for problem-solving are replaced by original ideas from students. When encouraged to think laterally, students are more likely to come up with unique ideas that are not usually found in the traditional classroom. This type of thinking requires students to construct meaning from an activity and to think like scientists.

Another benefit of experimentation is that it accommodates students' multiple intelligences. According to the theory of multiple intelligences, students possess many different aptitudes, but in varying degrees. Some of these forms of intelligence include linguistic, musical, logical-mathematical, spatial, kinesthetic, intrapersonal, and interpersonal. Learning is more likely to be acquired and retained when more than one sense is involved. During an experiment, students of all intellectual types find roles in which they can excel.

Students in the science classroom become involved in active learning, constructing new ideas based on their current knowledge and their experimental findings. The constructivist theory of learning encourages students to discover principles for and by themselves. Through problem solving and independent thinking, students build on what they know, moving forward in a manner that makes learning real and lasting.

Active, experimental learning makes connections between newly acquired information and the real world, a world that includes jobs. In the twenty-first century, employers expect their employees to identify and solve problems for themselves. Therefore, today's students, workers of the near future, will be required to use higher-level thinking skills. Experience with science experiments provides potential workers with the ability and confidence to be problem solvers.

The goal of Walker and Wood in *Facts On File Science Experiments* is to provide experiments that hook and hold the interest of students, teach basic concepts of science, and help students develop their critical-thinking skills. When fully immersed in an experiment, students can experience those "Aha!" moments, the special times when new information merges with what is already known and understanding breaks through. On these occasions, real and lasting learning takes place. The authors hope that this set of books helps bring more "Aha" moments into every science class.

Acknowledgments

This book would not exist were it not for our editor, Frank K. Darmstadt, who conceived and directed the project. Frank supervised the material closely, editing and making invaluable comments along the way. Betsy Feist of A Good Thing, Inc., is responsible for transforming our raw material into a polished and grammatically correct manuscript that makes us proud.

Introduction

All students ask "why?" because they really want to know how things work. The exploration of physical science, the study of natural processes in nonliving systems, is one way to find answers to some "why" questions about the world in which we live. Physical science is a foundational discipline in every student's science education. Chemistry and physics, two of the primary areas of physical science, are different but closely related fields. Physics encompasses the study of the world's fundamentals, from the tiniest particles to the framework of the universe. Chemistry focuses on the properties of matter and how individual atoms and molecules interact. Key to both physics and chemistry are the interactions between matter and energy, and how one can be created from the other.

Physical Science Experiments offers 20 new, engaging experiments and activities for students in grades 6 through 12. This volume is part of the new Facts On File Science Experiments set from Facts On File, Inc. The experiments included are original and appealing, providing teachers with fresh avenues for helping students understand the concepts of physical science. Teachers can rely on the experiments in this book to facilitate delivery of key science concepts while expanding students' learning experiences.

Experiments play many roles in science. Some are designed to teach particular concepts, some focus on a set of skills, and others promote critical thinking. All of the experiments in this book push students to expand their thinking. In each activity, students must reflect on the problem at hand rather than just carry out a set of procedures. Students are also asked how they might extend the experiment to learn more about the concept being taught. To help analyze their findings, students determine what sources of error may have come into play during the experiment.

The deepest, most meaningful learning in any science class takes place when students design and carry out their own experiments. This full-inquiry type of study requires students to pull from their own previous knowledge in order to solve new problems. A modification of this technique, partial inquiry, identifies a problem for students and asks them to solve it. Several of the experiments in *Physical Science Experiments* are based on the inquiry style of learning. Students are provided with appropriate materials and safety information and guided through the experimental process. In "Do All Carbonated Beverages Go Flat at the Same Rate?" students use knowledge of gas solubility to design their own experiment. "Which Materials Are the Best Sound Insulators?" prompts students to design experiments to find the best materials for damping sound. "Variables That Affect Speed" asks students to determine how variables affect the rate at which a ball rolls down a ramp.

Many of the experiments in this volume address issues of consumer science, bringing science out of the realm of theory and into everyday life. These kinds of experiments help students to get a glimpse of some applications of science. "Effectiveness of Plastic Wrap in Preventing Evaporation" explores characteristics of polymers that are found in plastic wrap products. Students apply titration skills to scrutinize how well fruit juices are labeled in "Accuracy of Labeling Vitamin C in Orange Juice." "The Relationship of Temperature to Viscosity" helps students understand the chemistry of motor oil. "Which Type of Food Contains the Most Energy?" uses a simple calorimeter to compare the caloric content of various snack foods. In "Does the Diameter of a Speaking Tube Affect Volume?" students look at the science of megaphones. Properties of lubricants are analyzed and compared in "What Are the Best Friction-Reducing Lubricants?" "Arrow Mass and Depth of Penetration" shows how mass affects the properties of arrows.

Two experiments focus on some of the basic concepts in all fields of science. Students learn about density and find out how the properties of matter vary depending on phase in "Comparing Densities of a Solid, Liquid, and Gas." To explore the relationship between surface area and volume, students can carry out the experiment "The Shape of an Ice Cube Affects Rate of Melting."

The relationship of matter and energy is a major theme in this book. Experiments that address this broad topic include "Graphing a Pendulum Swing," in which students experimentally determine how the length of a pendulum affects the frequency of its swing. In "Metals in Electromagnets," students find out how the core of an electromagnet affects its strength. "Which Fruits and Vegetables Make the Best Batteries?" has students use a galvanometer to test the conductivity of several fruit juices and analyze how a battery works. "Homemade Galvanometer" teaches principles of electricity and helps students understand how commercial galvanometers operate. In "How Does LED

Brightness Vary With Current?" students analyze the flow of electricity in varying types of circuits using LEDs. A calorimeter is used to compare the heat capacities of two metals in "The Heat Capacities of Zinc and Copper." The effect of shape on the conversion of kinetic to potential energy is addressed in "Does Shape Affect a Ball's Energy?" To understand how magnetic fields work and how they might be blocked, students carry out the experiment "Materials That Interfere With Magnetic Energy."

Like all of the activities in Facts On File Science Experiments, the activities in *Physical Science Experiments* are designed to help students delve into the big ideas of science and emerge with understanding. This book focuses on presenting complex physical science concepts in a style that is useful in grades 6 through 12. We hope that the next time physical science teachers hear "why?" questions in their classrooms, they will make use of this book to help students find the answers.

Safety Precautions

REVIEW BEFORE STARTING ANY EXPERIMENT

Each experiment includes special safety precautions that are relevant to that particular project. These do not include all the basic safety precautions that are necessary whenever you are working on a scientific experiment. For this reason, it is absolutely necessary that you read and remain mindful of the General Safety Precautions that follow. Experimental science can be dangerous and good laboratory procedure always includes following basic safety rules. Things can happen quickly while you are performing an experiment—for example, materials can spill, break, or even catch on fire. There will not be time after the fact to protect yourself. Always prepare for unexpected dangers by following the basic safety guidelines during the entire experiment, whether or not something seems dangerous to you at a given moment.

We have been quite sparing in prescribing safety precautions for the individual experiments. For one reason, we want you to take very seriously the safety precautions that are printed in this book. If you see it written here, you can be sure that it is here because it is absolutely critical.

Read the safety precautions here and at the beginning of each experiment before performing each lab activity. It is difficult to remember a long set of general rules. By rereading these general precautions every time you set up an experiment, you will be reminding yourself that lab safety is critically important. In addition, use your good judgment and pay close attention when performing potentially dangerous procedures. Just because the book does not say "Be careful with hot liquids" or "Don't cut yourself with a knife" does not mean that you can be careless when boiling water or using a knife to punch holes in plastic bottles. Notes in the text are special precautions to which you must pay special attention.

GENERAL SAFETY PRECAUTIONS

Accidents can be caused by carelessness, haste, or insufficient knowledge. By practicing safety procedures and being alert while conducting experiments, you can avoid taking an unnecessary risk. Be sure to check the individual experiments in this book for additional safety regulations and adult supervision requirements. If you will be working in a laboratory, do not work alone. When you are working off site, keep in groups with a minimum of three students per group, and follow school rules and state legal requirements for the number of supervisors required. Ask an adult supervisor with basic training in first aid to carry a small first-aid kit. Make sure everyone knows where this person will be during the experiment.

PREPARING

- Clear all surfaces before beginning experiments.
- Read the entire experiment before you start.
- Know the hazards of the experiments and anticipate dangers.

PROTECTING YOURSELF

- Follow the directions step by step.
- Perform only one experiment at a time.
- Locate exits, fire blanket and extinguisher, master gas and electricity shut-offs, eyewash, and first-aid kit.
- Make sure there is adequate ventilation.
- Do not participate in horseplay.
- Do not wear open-toed shoes.
- Keep floor and workspace neat, clean, and dry.
- Clean up spills immediately.
- If glassware breaks, do not clean it up by yourself; ask for teacher assistance.
- Tie back long hair.
- Never eat, drink, or smoke in the laboratory or workspace.
- Do not eat or drink any substances tested unless expressly permitted to do so by a knowledgeable adult.

USING EQUIPMENT WITH CARE

- Set up apparatus far from the edge of the desk.
- Use knives or other sharp, pointed instruments with care.

- Pull plugs, not cords, when removing electrical plugs.
- Clean glassware before and after use.
- Check glassware for scratches, cracks, and sharp edges.
- Let your teacher know about broken glassware immediately.
- Do not use reflected sunlight to illuminate your microscope.
- Do not touch metal conductors.
- Take care when working with any form of electricity.
- Use alcohol-filled thermometers, not mercury-filled thermometers.

USING CHEMICALS

- Never taste or inhale chemicals.
- Label all bottles and apparatus containing chemicals.
- Read labels carefully.
- Avoid chemical contact with skin and eyes (wear safety glasses or goggles, lab apron, and gloves).
- Do not touch chemical solutions.
- Wash hands before and after using solutions.
- Wipe up spills thoroughly.

HEATING SUBSTANCES

- Wear safety glasses or goggles, apron, and gloves when heating materials.
- Keep your face away from test tubes and beakers.
- When heating substances in a test tube, avoid pointing the top of the test tube toward other people.
- Use test tubes, beakers, and other glassware made of Pyrex™ glass.
- Never leave apparatus unattended.
- Use safety tongs and heat-resistant gloves.
- If your laboratory does not have heatproof workbenches, put your Bunsen burner on a heatproof mat before lighting it.
- Take care when lighting your Bunsen burner; light it with the airhole closed and use a Bunsen burner lighter rather than wooden matches.

- Turn off hot plates, Bunsen burners, and gas when you are done.
- Keep flammable substances away from flames and other sources of heat.
- Have a fire extinguisher on hand.

FINISHING UP

- Thoroughly clean your work area and any glassware used.
- Wash your hands.
- Be careful not to return chemicals or contaminated reagents to the wrong containers.
- Do not dispose of materials in the sink unless instructed to do so.
- Clean up all residues and put in proper containers for disposal.
- Dispose of all chemicals according to all local, state, and federal laws.

BE SAFETY CONSCIOUS AT ALL TIMES!

1. Accuracy of Labeling Vitamin C in Orange Juice

Topic

Vitamin C can be extracted from commercially prepared orange juice to check the accuracy of labeling.

Introduction

Vitamin C, also known as ascorbic acid (see Figure 1), is an essential nutrient in the human diet. Vitamin C is used in several metabolic processes and is a *cofactor* for many important enzymes in the body. In addition, vitamin C is a powerful *antioxidant* that helps protect the body from disease. Minor deficiencies in vitamin C can cause a multitude of side effects, and major deficiencies can result in *scurvy,* a disease characterized by tiredness, joint and muscle pain, and bleeding gums. Before the disease was understood, sailors who were at sea for several months would develop scurvy unless lemons and limes were on board. Because vitamin C is water soluble, it is not made by or stored in the body. Excess vitamin C cannot be saved in the tissues and is simply excreted in the urine, so this nutrient must be consumed daily as part of a healthy diet. Good dietary sources of vitamin C include fruits, such as strawberries and mangoes, and green vegetables, such as broccoli, leafy greens, and Brussels sprouts.

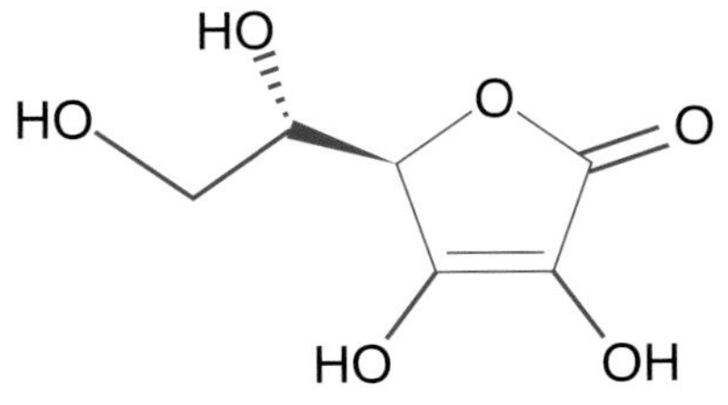

Figure 1

Chemical structure of ascorbic acid (vitamin C)

Because of the importance of vitamin C to a balanced diet, some food manufacturers add ascorbic acid to their products. Even though oranges contain a great deal of natural vitamin C, producers of orange juice commonly add ascorbic acid in order to raise the nutritional value. The amount of vitamin C in orange juice is reported on the nutrition label (see Figure 2). In this experiment, you will extract vitamin C from different brands of orange juice and compare the results to the amount listed on the nutrition label. You will use the technique of *titration*, a method of analysis used to find the exact quantity of a reactant in a titration flask. A burette is a calibrated tube with a stopcock that can be used to deliver a reactant to the flask (see Figure 3).

Nutrition Facts

Serving Size 8 fl oz (240 ml)
Serving Per Container 8

Amount Per Serving	
Calories 110	
	% Daily Value*
Total Fat 0g	0%
Sodium 0mg	0%
Potassium 450mg	13%
Total Carbohydrate 26g	9%
Sugars 22g	
Protein 2g	

Vitamin C	120%	●	Thiamin	10%
Niacin	4%	●	Folate	15%

Not a significant source of calories from fat, saturated fat, trans fat, cholesterol, dietary fiber. Vitaimin A, calcium and iron.

Percent Daily Values are based on a 2,000 calorie diet.

Figure 2

Sample nutrition label

Time Required

90 miniutes

Materials

➤ 4 different brands of orange juice with no pulp
➤ four 400-milliliter (ml) beakers
➤ stirring rod

- four 100- to 250-ml flasks
- burette
- ring stand with burette clamp
- 100-ml graduated cylinder
- 1 percent starch solution
- dropper
- Lugol's iodine solution
- labeling tape
- graph paper
- science notebook

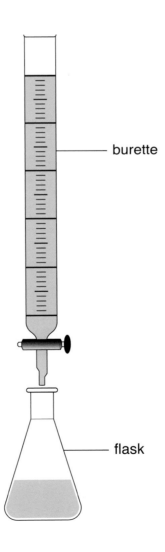

Figure 3

Safety Note Iodine will stain clothing and skin, so use extreme caution. Handle glassware carefully. Please review and follow the safety guidelines at the beginning of this volume.

Procedure

1. Obtain samples of four different brands of orange juice.
2. Examine the label of each brand of juice to find the amount of vitamin C listed per serving. Record this information on Data Table 1.
3. Answer Analysis questions 1 and 2.
4. Measure 100 ml of orange juice sample A using a graduated cylinder. Pour the sample into an Erlenmeyer flask. Label the flask as "A".
5. Add 10 drops of 1 percent starch solution into the flask.
6. Set up the burette on a ring stand in a burette clamp.
7. Fill the burette with Lugol's iodine solution. Record the starting reading, which is the level of iodine in the burette, under Trial 1 on Data Table 2.
8. Titrate the orange juice slowly. To do so, open the stopcock to add one drop of Lugol's iodine solution at a time, then swirl. Continue titrating until the solution in the flask turns a faint blue color that persists after swirling. When the blue color persists, you have reached the *endpoint*. (If the solution turns dark blue or purple, too much iodine has been added.) Record the level of iodine left in the burette, then calculate the amount of iodine used. Record the calculations on Data Table 2 under "Trial 1."
9. Repeat steps 4 through 8, using a fresh sample from the same container until you have two good (light blue) titrations. (You may need to carry out several trials to get two good titrations.)
10. Repeat steps 4 through 9 with the other three samples of orange juice.
11. Average the amount of iodine used to titrate the two best trials from each sample. Record the averages on Data Table 2.
12. Answer Analysis questions 3 through 7.

Analysis

1. According to the labels, which brand of orange juice has the most vitamin C?

Data Table 1	
Brand of orange juice	**Amount of vitamin C (from label)**
A. _____	
B. _____	
C. _____	
D. _____	

Data Table 2									
Brand	**Trial 1**		**Trial 2**		**Trial 3**		**Trial 4**		**Av. of two best trials**
	Readings start/end	**Am. of iodine**	**Readings start/end**	**Am. of iodine**	**Readings start/end**	**Am. of iodine**	**Readings start/end**	**Am. of iodine**	
A									
B									
C									
D									

2. Using the data from Data Table 1, create a bar graph comparing the amount of vitamin C in each of the four samples as indicated on the labels.

3. Which type of orange juice required the most iodine in the titration, and therefore had the most vitamin C?

4. Using the data from the average column of Data Table 2, create a bar graph comparing the amount of vitamin C according to your experimental results.

5. How do your experimental results compare to the amount of vitamin C listed on the orange juice nutrition labels?

6. What could have caused the discrepancies between the actual amount of vitamin C from the experiment and the amount listed on the labels?

7. List some sources of error in this experiment that may have affected your results.

What's Going On?

Titrations are performed to determine the unknown concentration of one substance using a substance with a known concentration. They are often done as *neutralization* reactions between an acid and a base. In this experiment, the ascorbic acid (vitamin C) in the orange juice reacted with the iodine that was titrated from the burette. As iodine reacted with ascorbic acid, the iodine molecules changed into colorless iodide ions. When all of the ascorbic acid had reacted with iodine, it began to react with the starch that was added to the orange juice, producing a blue-black starch-iodine complex. The slightly blue color of the solution at the titration endpoint indicated that all of the ascorbic acid had reacted. Therefore, the orange juice solution that required the most iodine in order to reach an endpoint had the highest quantity of vitamin C.

Ascorbic acid and iodine undergo an *oxidation/reduction* (or *redox*) *reaction*. This type of reaction always occurs in chemical pairs, with one chemical receiving electrons and another losing electrons. The molecule that loses electrons is *oxidized*, while the one that gains is *reduced*. During the reaction, the ascorbic acid lost electrons, which were transferred to the iodine molecule. The ascorbic acid was oxidized to dehydroascorbic acid while the iodine molecule gained electrons and was reduced to iodine ions.

Connections

Nutritional labels on food products in the United States must report the amount of certain nutrients, including vitamin C, in packaged food to the Food and Drug Administration (FDA). The FDA requires that nutrition labels on food packaging be accurate so the reported amounts of nutrients are tested frequently using methods much like the one used in this experiment. Most packaged foods are monitored by quality controllers directly after production. Nutrient values of most foods do not change very much from the time of production until purchase; therefore nutrition labels are very accurate. Vitamin C, however, is very reactive and breaks down easily with exposure to high temperatures, light, and water. Therefore, even if the amount of vitamin C is accurate during production, the actual amount that is in orange juice when it is consumed may vary depending on the shipping process and the length of time the juice is on the shelf at the supermarket.

Want to Know More?

See appendix for Our Findings.

Further Reading

American Chemical Society. "Ten-Year Study of Orange and Grapefruit Juice Yields Verdict on Vitamin C," 1997. Available online. URL: http://www.ultimatecitrus.com/pressrel.html. Accessed December 18, 2008. This press release summarizes the result of a study that found that because frozen concentrated orange juice is blended from many types of oranges, it has a relatively stable vitamin C concentration.

Dartmouth College. "ChemLab Titration," 1997–2000. Available online. URL: http://www.dartmouth.edu/~chemlab/techniques/titration.html. Accessed December 18, 2008. This Web site provides details on the technique of titrating.

Hubbard, Rosemary. "Vitamin C." Available online. URL: http://web1.caryacademy.org/chemistry/rushin/StudentProjects/CompoundWebSites/2001/AscorbicAcid/ascorbic.htm. Accessed December 18, 2008. This is a comprehensive Web site on vitamin C, providing history, chemical structure, and three dimensional models.

2. Graphing a Pendulum Swing

Topic

A graph can reveal information about the swing of a pendulum.

Introduction

A *pendulum* consists of a mass or *bob* that is connected to a fixed, pivoting point by a cord or rod. This simple device can swing in a rhythmic motion due to the force of gravity on the bob. As long as a force does not act against its motion, a pendulum will continue to swing. The constant swinging motion of a pendulum enables it to be used in measurements and timekeeping, as with pendulum clocks.

When a pendulum swings, the bob travels in an arc pattern (see Figure 1). Within the arc, there is a constant exchange between *potential* and *kinetic energy*. The potential energy is greatest when the pendulum is at either side of the arc. As the pendulum changes direction, it actually stops moving briefly and has no kinetic energy, only potential energy. When the pendulum bob is at the bottom of the arc, directly below the fixed pivot point, it has the greatest kinetic energy and the lowest potential energy.

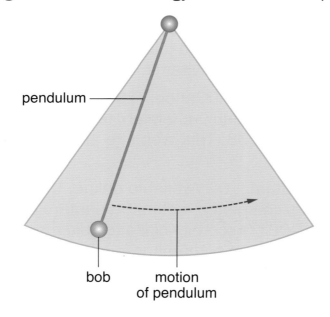

Figure 1

Two of the most important characteristics of a pendulum are its *period* and *frequency*. Period is the length of time it takes for the pendulum to make one swing back and forth. Frequency is how often it swings in a certain amount of time. Period and frequency are related; the longer the period of a pendulum, the lower its frequency. Similarly, the shorter the period of a pendulum, the higher its frequency. In this experiment, you will create pendulums with cords of varying lengths and graph their movement to analyze frequency.

Time Required

30 minutes on part A
45 minutes on part B

Materials

- piece of string 100 centimeters (cm) (39.4 inches [in.]) long
- tape
- scissors
- ruler
- large fishing weight or mass with a hook
- protractor
- stopwatch or clock with a second hand
- graph paper
- science notebook

Safety Note   Please review and follow the safety guidelines at the beginning of this volume.

Procedure, Part A

1. Answer Analysis question 1.
2. To create a pendulum, attach one end of a string to a fishing weight or similar mass. Tape the other end of the string to the edge of a table or desk so that it swings freely. Measure the string so that there is 90 cm (35.4 in.) between the mass and the pivot point, the point where the string drops from the table or desk.

3. Hold a protractor so that the flat side is against the bottom edge of the desk or table and the string lines up at 90 degrees when the pendulum is at rest. Pull the bob to one side so that the string is at a 15-degree angle (according to the protractor) and let it swing.

4. Using a stopwatch to monitor time, count the number of swings made by the pendulum in one minute. Record the time on the data table.

5. Repeat steps 1 through 4 using pendulums made with 70, 50, 30, and 10 cm (27.6, 19.7, 11.2, and 3.9 in.) strings.

6. Calculate the period length of each pendulum by dividing the number of swings by 60 seconds (sec). Record the period length on the data table.

7. Answer Analysis questions 2 through 5.

Data Table		
Pendulum length in centimeters	**Number of swings in 1 minute**	**Period length**
90		
70		
50		
30		
10		

Procedure, Part B

1. Design an experiment to find out how changing the mass of the bob affects the period length.

2. Answer Analysis question 6.

3. Show your design to your teacher. If your teacher approves, perform the experiment.

4. Answer Analysis question 7.

Analysis

1. Write a hypothesis predicting how you think pendulum length will affect the frequency of pendulum swings.

2. What forces are acting on the pendulum as it swings?

3. In a vacuum, a pendulum would continue to swing indefinitely. However, the pendulum you created will eventually slow to a stop. Why is this?

4. Using the data from the data table, create a line graph comparing the length of the pendulum to the frequency of its swings.

5. How does pendulum length affect its frequency? Why is this so?

6. Write a hypothesis predicting how you think the mass of the pendulum bob will affect the frequency of pendulum swings.

7. Did your experiment support or disprove your hypothesis?

What's Going On?

The period of a pendulum's swing (T) depends on the following equation:

$$T = 2\pi \sqrt{(L/g)}$$

where g represents the pull of gravity (9.8 m/sec^2) and L is the length of the pendulum in meters. Therefore, the length of time a pendulum takes to make one swing depends on the length of the pendulum and the pull of gravity. A longer string will result in a longer period, while a shorter string produces a shorter period. The mass of the pendulum bob is not included in the equation because it is not relevant to the swing of a pendulum.

Newton's second law of motion states that every object in motion will continue in motion until acted upon by a force. A pendulum will continue to swing in its arclike pattern until it is acted upon by a force that causes it to stop. The force that causes a pendulum to stop is *friction*. Although one cannot see the molecules and particles that exist in air, they create resistance that causes a pendulum to slow down and eventually stop. Heavier pendulum bobs are not slowed down as much as lighter ones because of the energy in their swing. Although mass does not affect the period of a swinging pendulum, it does affect the energy of the pendulum. More massive pendulum bobs have a greater quantity of potential and kinetic energy and are therefore less affected by air resistance.

Connections

A *Foucault pendulum* is a special type of pendulum that demonstrates the rotation of the Earth on its axis. This type of pendulum was named after its creator, the French physicist Jean-Bernard-Leon Foucault (1819–68). A Foucault pendulum consists of a large bob suspended from a fixed point so that it has a 360-degree range of motion. As a Foucault pendulum swings, it appears to change its rotation slightly over time. Often, these pendulums are set up so that they will trace a path in sand as they swing so that the Earth's motion can be observed.

Although it may appear that the plane in which a Foucault pendulum moves shifts slightly over time, it does not. A Foucault pendulum actually maintains its original trajectory. However, the Earth rotates underneath the pendulum. If a Foucault pendulum were placed on the north or south pole, it would trace an absolute circular path over a 24-hour day (see Figure 2). The motion path varies at other latitudes, and does not rotate at all at the equator.

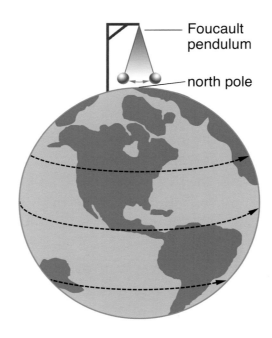

Figure 2

Motion of a Foucault pendulum at the north pole

Want to Know More?

See appendix for Our Findings.

Further Reading

Matthews, Michael. "The International Pendulum Project: An Overview." Available online. URL: http://www.arts.unsw.edu.au/pendulum/about. html. Accessed December 18, 2008. The Web page examines the history of the study of pendulum motion.

Neuman, Erik. "My Physics Lab: Simple Pendulum." Available online. URL: http://www.myphysicslab.com/pendulum1.html. Accessed March 16, 2009. Neuman offers a Java applet and detailed explanation of the physics of pendulums.

Physclips. "The Foucault Pendulum." The Australian Learning and Teaching Council. Available online. URL: http://www.physclips.unsw.edu.au/jw/foucault_pendulum.html. Accessed December 18, 2008. This Web page shows a Foucault pendulum in motion and explains its behavior.

3. Metals in Electromagnets

Topic

Experiments can determine the effectiveness of three different metals in electromagnets.

Introduction

Any time an electrical current passes through a wire, the current emits a small magnetic force. A wire wrapped many times around a metal core such as a nail creates an *electromagnet* (see Figure 1). Electromagnets are similar to normal magnets, such as those that attach to your refrigerator. However, electromagnets may be turned on and off by regulating the flow of electricity through the wire. The strength of an electromagnet is influenced by the number of times the wire is wrapped around the metal core, as well as by the type of metal used as the core.

An electrical *current*, essentially the transfer of electrons, is required for an electromagnet. One easy-to-use source of electrical current is a battery. Electrons flow from the negative end of a battery and are transferred to the positive end through a conductive wire, such as copper. Wire carrying a current will create a small magnetic force, but the magnetic attraction increases greatly when the wire is wrapped around a core, such as a nail, made of metal.

In this experiment, you will design and carry out a procedure to create electromagnets using three different metal cores. As in all good experiments, you will need to control for variables in the procedure you design. For example, in all of your trials, use the same type and length of wire, as well as the same amount of current.

 **Time Required**

60 minutes

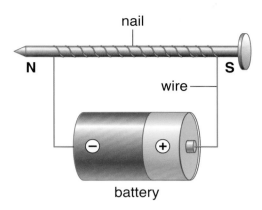

Figure 1

Electromagnet

Materials

- D-cell battery
- insulated copper wire (22 gauge) (about 12 inch [in.] [30 centimeters (cm)])
- pair of wire strippers/cutters
- iron nail (3 in. [7.5 cm])
- steel nail (3 in. [7.5 cm])
- aluminum nail (3 in. [7.5 cm])
- zinc alloy nail (3 in. [7.5 cm])
- package of staples
- ruler
- graph paper
- science notebook

Safety Note   Use caution when working with sharp metal wire and tools, such as wire strippers. Please review and follow the safety guidelines at the beginning of this volume.

Procedure

1. Your job is to design and perform an experiment to find out which of the metals supplied to you is the most effective when used in an electromagnet.

2. You can use any of the supplies provided by your teacher, but you may not need to use all of them.

3. Before you conduct your experiment, decide exactly what you are going to do. Write the steps you plan to take (your experimental procedure) and the materials you plan to use (materials list) on the data table. Show your procedure and materials list to the teacher. If you get teacher approval, proceed with your experiment. If not, modify your work and show it to your teacher again.

4. Once you have teacher approval, assemble the materials you need and begin your procedure.

5. Collect your results on a data table of your own design.

Data Table	
Your experimental procedure	
Your materials list	
Teacher's approval	

Analysis

1. In your procedure, what factors did you control to ensure that the experimental data was accurate?

2. How did you determine which electromagnet was the strongest?

3. Which type of metal produced the strongest electromagnet? The weakest?

4. Why do you think that some metals make better electromagnets than others?

5. Why did the wire have to be attached to the battery in order for the electromagnet to work?

What's Going On?

The attractive forces of a magnet are produced when all of the electrons in the atoms of the magnet are spinning in the same direction. The movement of electrons in a single atom creates a very small *electromagnetic field.* Generally, electrons in a metal spin in random directions. Throughout the metal the magnetic spins of atoms cancel each other out. However, when most of the atoms in a substance align their electrons to spin in the same direction, they create one big magnetic field.

In a regular bar magnet, electrons are aligned so that the magnet has two opposite poles, one that is positively charged, and another with a negative charge (see Figure 2). However, in an electromagnet, the charged poles only exist when there is a current of electrons passing through the piece of metal. Copper wire is used in electromagnets because it is an excellent conductor of electricity. The core of an electromagnet does not necessarily have to be a good conductor; however, it must have electrons that will easily align with each other.

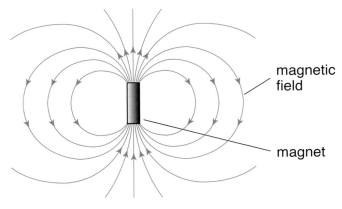

magnetic field

magnet

Figure 2

Some metals are made up of *domains*, small regions within which all electrons are spinning the same direction. Generally, domains are randomly oriented, but if they are exposed to a magnetic field, they will align and the piece of metal will produce a strong magnetic field. Iron and steel have larger domains than metals, such as aluminum and brass, and are generally capable of making stronger electromagnets.

Connections

Have you ever relied a compass to find your way? A compass uses the Earth's magnetic force to point travelers in the correct direction. The Earth has magnetic north and south poles that are close to the location of the geographic north and south poles. A compass needle (or any other magnet with equal and oppositely charged poles) will align so that it points toward magnetic north. After determining which direction is north, a traveler can find any other of the *cardinal directions*, south, east, or west.

The Earth's magnetic poles are a result of the movement of the molten iron at the core of the planet. The Earth's core consists mostly of iron that is heated to extreme temperatures. The cooler metal at the outside of the core produces an electrical field due to the movement of the liquid core. This electrical field causes the Earth to have a net movement of electrons, forming distinct poles. Magnetic north can be found at the center of the Arctic sea, which is usually covered by ice. The magnetic South Pole is located in Antarctica.

 ## Want to Know More?

See appendix for Our Findings.

Further Reading

Brain, Marshall. "How Compasses Work," HowStuffWorks, 2009. Available online. URL: http://www.howstuffworks.com/compass.htm. Accessed July 7, 2009. In this article, Brian explains how compasses use magnetic fields to find locate the north pole and tells how compasses are made and work.

Brain, Marshall. "How Electromagnets Work," HowStuffWorks, 2009. Available online. URL: http://science.howstuffworks.com/electromagnet2.htm. Accessed January 1, 2009. Brain explains how electric currents produce magnetic fields and provides an animation.

Cornell University. "Getting down to the core of electromagnets," June 12, 2002. Available online. URL: http://www.ccmr.cornell.edu/education/ask/index.html?quid=635. Accessed December 19, 2008. Cornell scientists answer questions about electromagnets and related topics.

Stern, David P. "The Self-Sustaining Dynamo in the Earth's Core, Origin of The Earth's Magnetism," February 23, 2008. Available online. URL: http://www.phy6.org/earthmag/dynamos2.htm. Accessed December 19, 2008. Stern provides a detailed explanation of the Earth's magnetic field.

4. Effectiveness of Plastic Wrap in Preventing Evaporation

Topic

Not all types of plastic wrap show the same effectiveness at preventing evaporation.

Introduction

Food is often covered with plastic wrap, as shown in Figure 1, in order to keep it fresh and to prevent spills. The first type of plastic wrap ever used was *cellophane.* Jacques Brandenberger (1872–1954), a Swiss textile engineer, invented cellophane in 1908, and production for home use began in the mid-1930s. Cellophane is made of *cellulose*, a long, strong fiber made by plants. Soon after the widespread production of cellophane, scientists researched other ways to produce plastic film that would reduce exposure of foods to air and conditions that affect their quality.

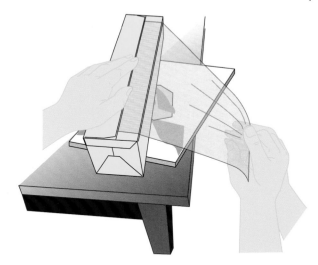

Figure 1

Household plastic wrap

Today, many different types of plastic wrap are commonly used in households. The three most popular types are *polyethylene*, which is used in Glad™ brand plastic wrap, *polyvinyl chloride*, used in Reynolds™ plastic wrap, and *polyvinylidene chloride*, used in Saran™ wrap. Because these types of plastic wrap are made from different materials, their properties are slightly different. In this laboratory, you will perform a test to determine which material is the most effective at preventing water evaporation.

Time Required

60 minutes

Materials

- three 250-milliliter (ml) beakers
- 3 rubber bands
- 3 types of plastic wrap (Saran™ wrap, Glad™ wrap, and Reynolds™ wrap)
- large hot plate
- 300 ml of deionized water
- labeling tape
- hot mitts
- goggles
- graph paper
- science notebook

Safety Note Use caution when working with hot plates and when using water near electrical outlets. Wear goggles and use hot mitts to move beakers after they are heated on the hot plates. Please review and follow the safety guidelines at the beginning of this volume.

Procedure

1. Label three beakers to reflect the type of wrap that will be used on them ("Saran," "Glad," and "Reynolds").
2. Fill one beaker with 100 ml of deionized water.
3. Cut a piece of the brand of plastic wrap specified on the beaker so that it will completely cover the top of the beaker.

4. Cover the beaker with the plastic wrap and secure it with a rubber band.

5. Repeat steps 2 through 4 with the two remaining beakers and types of plastic wrap.

6. Place all three beakers on a large hot plate. Turn the hot plate setting on low.

7. Heat the beakers for 30 minutes. While you are waiting, answer Analysis questions 1 and 2.

8. Allow the beakers to cool before handling. Tap the beakers lightly to allow any condensed water on the plastic wrap to return to the bottom of the beaker.

9. Record the level of the water in each beaker on the data table.

10. Subtract the amount of water remaining in each beaker from 100 ml to determine the amount of water that evaporated. Record this information on the data table.

11. Answer Analysis questions 3 through 6.

Data Table		
Type of plastic wrap	Amount of water remaining	Amount of water evaporated
Glad™ Wrap		
Reynolds™ Wrap		
Saran™ Wrap		

Analysis

1. Describe the physical characteristics of each of the three types of plastic wrap. Include differences in appearance, thickness, texture, and flexibility.

2. Which type of plastic wrap do you predict will be the most effective at preventing evaporation? The least? Justify your answer.

3. Create a bar graph comparing the amount of water that evaporated from each beaker, using the information recorded on the data table.

4. In this experiment, which type of plastic wrap was the most effective at preventing evaporation?

5. Do these results agree with your prediction from Analysis question 2? Why or why not?

6. If one brand of plastic wrap is best at preventing water loss, why do you think that there are so many different types of plastic wrap available for purchase?

What's Going On?

Water exists in three different forms: solid, liquid, and gas. Generally, at room temperature, water tends to remain in the liquid form. However, the air can hold a great deal of water vapor (water in the gaseous form) at room temperature as well. Condensation of water vapor in the air is responsible for the formation of clouds and for the droplets that occur on the outside of a cold glass. Water continually vaporizes and condenses, creating a constant change of states between liquid and gas known as a *water cycle*. Evaporation can be accelerated by boiling. When water boils, molecules move faster than usual and are more likely to break free from the forces that hold them together.

In the liquid state, water molecules are relatively close together. Heating causes water molecules to move rapidly and spread apart, increasing the likelihood that the molecules will travel through surfaces that are usually impermeable, such as plastic wrap. Although plastic wrap is designed to prevent spills, spoilage, and the evaporation of water, there are tiny holes between the fibers that make up the wrap. These holes give the material some flexibility. Some types of plastic wrap contain more or bigger holes than others. This increased porosity may allow more water to pass through.

Connections

Although plastic wrap has been used in households for many years, there is a great deal of environmental concern surrounding its popularity. First, the chemical processes used to create plastic wrap creates a by-product that cannot be broken down and causes environmental pollution. In addition, plastic wrap itself is difficult, if not impossible, to recycle because it is intended to be used once and thrown away. Therefore, plastic wrap creates waste that is not *biodegradable*.

In addition to environmental concerns, many brands of plastic wrap contain "plasticizers" that make them more flexible. Polyvinyl chloride tends to have the greatest percentage of plasticizers, up to 30 percent. Polyvinylidene chloride generally has 10 percent plasticizers, and polyethylene does not have any. Plasticizers may be absorbed by food when it is heated, and then may be consumed by humans. Some scientists are concerned that the consumption of such plasticizers may cause several health problems.

Want to Know More?

See appendix for Our Findings.

Further Reading

Answers.com. "Plastic Wrap," 2008. Available online. URL: http://www.answers.com/topic/plastic-wrap. Accessed January 8, 2008. This article contains detailed information on the structure and manufacture of plastic wrap.

Chem4kids.com. "Evaporation of Liquids," 2007. Available online. URL: http://www.chem4kids.com/files/matter_evap.html. Accessed January 8, 2009. This Web site explains the relationship between energy and rate of evaporation.

History of Science. "Assignment 5: Jacques Edwin Brandenberger," April 6, 2008. Available online. URL: http://historyofscience2008.blogspot.com/2008/04/assignment-5-jacques-edwin.html. Accessed December 19, 2008. This Web site provides a concise account of Brandenberger's work in the development of plastic wrap as well as some good references for further study.

5. Which Fruits and Vegetables Make the Best Batteries?

Topic

Fruits and vegetables can be used to make weak batteries.

Introduction

Many of the things we use on a daily basis are powered by batteries, including cars, cell phones, watches, and remote controls. Batteries provide power to electronic devices by supplying them with a current of electrons. In a battery, electrons flow from the negative terminal, known as the *anode*, to the positive terminal, the *cathode*. If the two nodes of a battery are connected directly to each other, electrons will flow very quickly from one end to the other, draining the battery of its power. However, if the flow of electrons is directed through some type of device, such as a clock or phone, they can be harnessed to do work.

Any type of *electrolyte* solution can provide a source of power for a battery. An electrolyte is a liquid that readily reacts with metal electrodes to transfer electron. Batteries can be created using many different types of fruits and vegetables by inserting electron donating and accepting metal electrodes. If the electrodes are attached to a circuit using conductive wire, the fruit or vegetable can potentially power a clock for several days. In this experiment, you will determine which type of fruit or vegetable creates the best battery.

Time Required

60 minutes

Materials

- •→ zinc-plated nail (or similar piece of zinc metal)
- •→ thick piece of nail-length copper wire (or similar piece of copper metal)

- 2 wire connectors with alligator clips
- lemon
- potato
- 2 other types of fruit or vegetables
- galvanometer
- science notebook

Safety Note   Do not eat any of the fruits or vegetables that have been used as batteries. Although low voltages will be passing through the wires, use caution when working with electric currents. Please review and follow the safety guidelines at the beginning of this volume.

Procedure

1. Answer Analysis questions 1 and 2.
2. Choose a fruit or vegetable. Insert a piece of zinc into one end of the fruit or vegetable and a piece of copper into the opposite end.
3. Clip a wire connector to the zinc electrode. Clip the other wire connector to the copper electrode.
4. Attach the free end of the wire connected to the zinc electrode to the negative terminal of the galvanometer. Attach the free end of the wire connected to the copper electrode to the positive terminal (see Figure 1). You have created a fruit battery.
5. Record the galvanometer reading for the fruit battery on the data table.
6. Repeat steps 2 through 5 with each type of fruit or vegetable.
7. Answer Analysis questions 3 through 6.

Data Table				
Type of fruit or vegetable				
Galvanometer reading				

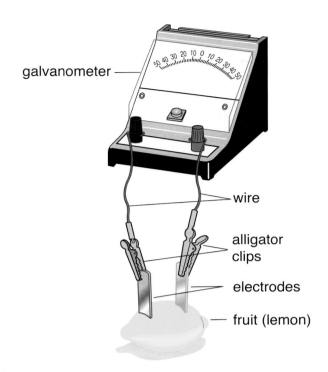

galvanometer

wire

alligator clips

electrodes

fruit (lemon)

Figure 1

Fruit battery

Analysis

1. Which types of fruits or vegetables did you choose to test in the experiment? Explain why you chose them.

2. Write a hypothesis describing which fruit or vegetable "battery" you think will produce the greatest electric current. Explain your reasoning.

3. Copper gives up electrons easily whereas zinc attracts electrons. Which piece of metal in your battery serves as the cathode? The anode? Why is this so?

4. What would happen if you used two pieces of the same type of metal as electrodes in the battery?

5. Which type of fruit or vegetable produced the best battery? The worst?

6. What characteristics of the fruit/vegetable named in Analysis question 5 made it a good battery?

What's Going On?

The juices of most fruits and vegetables are electrolytes, solutions that contain *ions*. Ionic solutions, such as acids or bases, contain charged particles that will transfer electrons and therefore conduct electricity. Since most fruits and vegetables are at least slightly acidic, they will produce some kind of voltage under the right circumstances.

In a fruit/vegetable battery such as the ones created in this lab, the electrolyte solution reacts with the metal electrodes. Copper acts as a cathode; it readily donates electrons, causing it to have a positive charge. Zinc accepts electrons and becomes the negatively charged anode. Electrons travel from the anode to the cathode, which produces an electrical current. Stronger electrolytes produce more electrons. Highly acidic solutions are strong electrolytes, so acidic fruits such as lemons and limes tend to make the best batteries.

Connections

Most electrical devices require more than one battery in order to function. A single battery only has a limited number of electrons that can be donated into an electrical current. In order to increase the efficiency of the electron flow, several batteries may be linked together in a *circuit.* If the positive terminal of one battery is connected to the negative terminal of another battery, the electrical current produced will be doubled. Multiple-battery circuits are commonly used in order to magnify the electrical current produced by a single battery alone (see Figure 2).

If you look inside a flashlight or a CD player, you will most likely find alkaline or zinc batteries. Both types of batteries have a cathode and an anode, but their positions are reversed. In a zinc chloride battery, the cathode is inside the battery and the anode is the battery exterior. The reverse is true in alkaline batteries, in which the anode is the material on the inside and the cathode is on the outside. In the factory, alkaline battery cathodes are made up of graphite, manganese dioxide, and an electrolyte that is pressed into a tubular pellet. The pellet is inserted into a small steel canister. The anode, which is made up of a gel that contains zinc powder, is inserted inside the cathode pellet, with a paper separating the two. A brass nail on the top acts as a current collect. Once everything is in place, the battery is sealed to keep it from losing its charge.

Want to Know More?

See appendix for Our Findings.

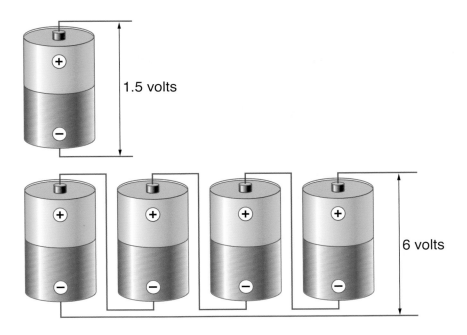

Figure 2

A muliple-battery circuit produces more voltage than a simple battery.

Further Reading

Battery Education. "How Do Batteries Work?" August 24, 2006. Available online. URL: http://www.batteryeducation.com/2006/08/how_do_ batterie.html. Accessed January 8, 2009. Battery Education provides basic information on battery technology, battery uses, and the technical aspects of batteries.

British Broadcasting Cooperation. "The Open University." Available online. URL: http://www.open2.net/science/. Accessed January 8, 2009. Supported by the BBC, this Web site provides information on batteries and other topics in science.

Green-Planet-Solar-Energy.com, "How Do Batteries Work?" January 4, 2009. Available online. URL: http://www.green-planet-solar-energy.com/ how-do-batteries-work.html. Accessed January 8, 2009. This Web site discusses lead acid, nickel cadmium, and nickel hybrid batteries.

6. Do All Carbonated Beverages Go Flat at the Same Rate?

Topic

Dissolved carbon dioxcide comes out of solution until equilibrium is reached.

Introduction

Have you ever poured yourself a glass of your favorite soda, then taken a sip and realized that it has gone flat? Soft drinks simply do not taste the same without the fizz of carbonation. Manufacturers dissolve carbon dioxide (see Figure 1) in beverages under pressurized conditions. Along with fizz, carbonation also provides a pleasant, sharp taste that comes from the carbonic acid formed when carbon dioxide mixes with water under pressure. The equation for this reaction is:

$$H_2O + CO_2 \leftrightarrow H_2CO_3$$

water + carbon dioxide ↔ carbonic acid

The bubbles in a carbonated beverage are caused by carbon dioxide escaping from the liquid in which they were dissolved. Carbonated drinks

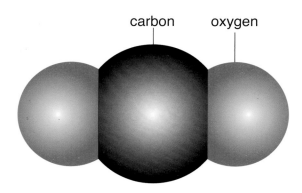

Figure 1

Structure of carbon dioxide

are generally sealed in a bottle or a can under high pressure until they are ready for consumption. As soon as the beverage is opened and the pressure is released, carbon dioxide begins to escape from the solution. That is why you hear a hissing sound as you open a bottle of soda. Carbon dioxide will continue to escape from the liquid until it reaches equilibrium with the atmosphere. At this point, your drink will not bubble anymore and is "flat." In this laboratory, you will design an experiment to determine if some types of carbonated beverages go flat faster than others.

Time Required

55 minutes

Materials

- 5 different types of carbonated beverages (all in the same size bottle)
- balloons
- rubber bands
- electronic scale or triple-beam balance
- thermometer
- stopwatch
- measuring tape (the flexible type)
- graph paper
- science notebook

Safety Note   Please review and follow the safety guidelines at the beginning of this volume.

Procedure

1. Your job is to design and perform an experiment to find out which type of soft drink loses the most carbonation over time.
2. You can use any of the supplies provided by your teacher, but you may not need to use all of them.

3. Before you conduct your experiment, decide exactly what you are going to do. Keep these points in mind:

    a. You need to develop a way to capture and measure the carbon dioxide gas released by each beverage.

    b. Your experiment should be controlled. For example, if you collect carbon dioxide gas from one container at room temperature, you must collect from all containers at the same temperature. Or, if you shake one container before collecting the gas, you must shake all the containers. Likewise, if you collect gas from one container for 5 minutes, you must do the same with the other containers.

    Write the steps you plan to take (your experimental procedure) and the materials you plan to use (materials list) on the data table. Show your procedure and materials list to the teacher. If you get teacher approval, proceed with your experiment. If not, modify your work and show it to your teacher again.

4. Once you have teacher approval, assemble the materials you need and begin your procedure.

5. Collect your results on a data table of your own design.

Analysis

1. Describe the characteristics of the five beverages that were tested. How were they different in terms of color, brand, type of sweetener, and other factors?

2. What steps did you include in your procedure to ensure that this was a controlled experiment?

3. How did you make sure that you accounted for all of the gas released from the beverage (and that none leaked out without being measured)?

4. Create a bar graph comparing the amount carbon dioxide released from each type of beverage.

5. Which beverage lost the greatest amount of carbon dioxide over the specified period of time?

6. What factors do you think influence the amount of carbon dioxide released by a beverage?

7. Did all of the beverages contain equal amounts of carbon dioxide? How do you know?

Data Table	
Your experimental procedure	
Your materials list	
Teacher's approval	

What's Going On?

Two factors affect the solubility of gases such as carbon dioxide in liquids: temperature and pressure. A gas dissolves more easily in a liquid at low temperatures, so manufacturers chill beverages before introducing carbon dioxide gas. In addition, when air pressure is high, gases dissolve more readily than they do at normal pressure (see Figure 2). Bottling companies pressurize beverages so they can easily introduce large volumes of carbon dioxide. Some types of carbonated beverages contain more carbon dioxide than others. Seltzer waters and soft drinks with artificial sweeteners tend to contain more carbonation than sugar-containing soft drinks. Additional carbon dioxide simply produces more carbonic acid, giving the drink its desired taste.

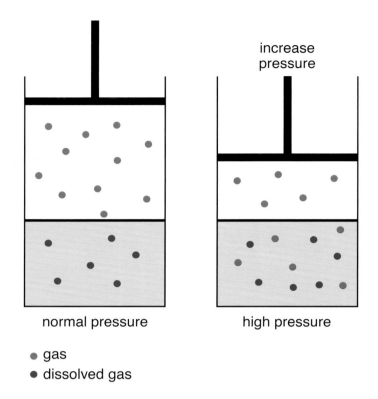

Figure 2

A fluid holds more dissolved gas when pressure is high.

Carbon dioxide is generally a gas at room temperature and standard pressure. Therefore, as soon as a carbonated beverage container loses its high pressure, carbon dioxide begins to diffuse out of solution. Two factors increase the rate at which carbon dioxide comes out of solution: high temperatures and shaking. To maintain dissolved carbon dioxide, it is best to keep the beverage cool. In addition, avoid shaking the beverage. Shaking increases the surface area of the beverages, increasing the interaction of the beverage with air.

Connections

People have been drinking naturally carbonated mineral waters for hundreds of years because of their supposed healing properties. Carbonated water can occur in nature due to the chemical reactions that take place in some natural springs or in caves. Man-made mineral water was first produced in the late 1700s, but it was not commonly packaged for consumption until the mid-1800s. After this time, mineral water, or soda water as it was known, became increasingly popular, and was soon combined with noncarbonated soft drinks to create different flavors.

The popularity of flavored mineral water led to the development of drinks such as ginger ale, root beer, and eventually Coca Cola™, Dr. Pepper™, and Pepsi Cola™. These beverages have become increasingly popular around the world since their invention. Today, there are hundreds of types of carbonated soft drinks in different brands, flavors, and varieties. However, unlike the original carbonated beverages, soft drinks today are marketed for their taste, not for their health benefits.

Want to Know More?

See appendix for Our Findings.

Further Reading

Ask a Scientist. "Measuring Carbonation," January 20, 2006. Available online. URL: http://www.newton.dep.anl.gov/askasci/chem03/chem03713.htm. Accessed February 17, 2009. The writer of this Web page suggests some ways to measure the amount of carbon dioxide gas given off by a carbonated beverage.

Edinformatics. "Soft drink," 1999. Available online. URL: http://www.edinformatics.com/inventions_inventors/soft_drinks.htm. Accessed February 17, 2009. This Web page provides information on several different types of carbonated drinks and discusses the names of these beverages in different countries.

The History of Pop Timeline. "Introduction to Pop," 2009. Available online. URL: http://inventors.about.com/library/weekly/aa091699.htm. Accessed February 17, 2009. Major events in the development of carbonated drinks are outlined on this Web site.

7. The Shape of an Ice Cube Affects Rate of Melting

Topic

The shape of a mass of ice affects the rate at which it melts.

Introduction

When you ask for a soft drink or glass of water at a restaurant, you expect to find ice in the beverage. Ice cools drinks by absorbing some of the heat they contain. As a result of this transfer of heat, the ice melts. Once all of the ice in a beverage has melted, the temperature of the drink rises until it reaches room temperature. Very small pieces of ice will cool a drink quickly, but they also melt quickly. Large pieces of ice do not chill a drink as rapidly as small ones, but they will remain frozen for a longer period of time. The more slowly an ice cube melts, the longer it will keep a drink cool.

Ice cubes are simply small pieces of water in the solid form. When water is cooled below its freezing point (32 degrees Fahrenheit [°F] or 0 degrees Celsius [°C]), it crystallizes into ice. As with all liquids, water takes the form of the container in which it is placed. Therefore, ice cubes can easily be formed into many different shapes and sizes. In this experiment, you will test ice cubes made from the same volume of water in different shapes to determine if shape affects rate of melting.

Time Required

15 minutes on day 1
overnight for ice cubes to form
60 minutes on day 2

Materials

- 300 milliliters (ml) distilled water
- graduated cylinder

36

- access to a freezer
- 6 different small plastic molds (for making shaped ice cubes or gelatin)
- plastic wrap
- 6 small bowls
- 12 labels
- waterproof labeling pen
- graph paper
- science notebook

Safety Note Please review and follow the safety guidelines at the beginning of this volume.

Procedure, Day 1

1. Measure 50 ml of distilled water. (The volume can be altered depending on the size of the plastic molds, as long as it is constant for all molds.)
2. Pour the water into a plastic mold, ensuring that none spills.
3. Cover the mold with plastic wrap.
4. Repeat steps 1 through 3 with the remaining 5 molds. Label each mold with a letter (A through F).
5. Place the molds in the freezer and allow them to solidify overnight. Be careful not to spill any water while transporting the molds.
6. Answer Analysis questions 1 and 2.

Procedure, Day 2

1. Label the six bowls with a letter (A through F).
2. Remove the molds from the freezer.
3. Remove each ice cube from its mold by turning it upside down over the bowl labeled with the corresponding letter. Press gently on the bottom of the tray until the ice cube pops out.
4. After all of the ice cubes are placed in their bowls, record the experiment "Start time" on the data table.

5. Allow the ice cubes to melt completely. After an ice cube has melted completely, record the time on the data table.

6. Answer Analysis questions 3 through 8.

Data Table			
Ice shape	Start time	Finish time	Time required to melt (Finish time – Start time)
A			
B			
C			
D			
E			
F			

Analysis

1. Which shapes did you choose for your ice cubes?

2. Write a hypothesis predicting which of your ice cubes will melt the fastest and which one will melt the slowest. Justify your choices.

3. Which ice cube melted first? Last?

4. Create a bar graph comparing the amount of time (in minutes) it took for each ice cube to melt completely.

5. What factors do you think affected the speed at which the ice cubes melted?

6. Why was it important to use the same volume of water in each mold?

7. If you were going to produce a type of ice cube that would be advertised as "the slowest melting ice cube," what shape would it be?

8. Describe some sources of error in this experiment that may have affected your experimental results.

What's Going On?

The rate at which ice melts depends on the ratio of its *surface area* to its volume. The surface area of an object is the amount of area that is exposed to the outside atmosphere. The surface area of a regular-shaped object can be found by adding the areas of each side of the object. All the ice cubes in this experiment had the same volume, so the rate of melting depended solely on the surface area of each cube. An ice cube with a small surface area will remain frozen for a longer period of time than one of the same volume with a large surface area.

Ice melts because it absorbs heat from its surroundings. When solid water absorbs heat energy, the water molecules begin moving. This motion dislodges the molecules from their solid crystalline form (see Figure 1). Therefore, there is a direct relationship between the number of molecules exposed to warm air or water and the rate at which heat is absorbed.

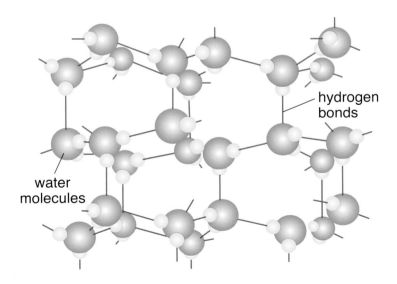

Figure 1

Crystalline form of ice

Connections

Water is continuously recycled on Earth through a series of events known as the *water cycle* (see Figure 2). Water *evaporates* from the land and surface water, *condenses* in the air to form clouds, then falls as *precipitation*. Most of the water on Earth is saltwater, leaving only 3 percent freshwater, the water on which all living things rely. Three-quarters of the freshwater is frozen as polar ice, thick sheets found at the north and south poles. At the north pole, floating pack ice covers about 108 million square feet (million ft^2) (10 million square kilometers [million km^2]). Antarctica, the land mass at the south pole, is covered by a thick ice sheet that covers about 151 million ft^2 (14 million km^2) of ice. Despite the fact that these regions are gigantic, very old, tightly packed masses of ice, they have been melting in recent years due to increased global temperatures. Thickening layers of carbon dioxide and other *greenhouse gases*, the products of fossil fuel combustion, are trapping heat near the Earth and raising air and water temperatures.

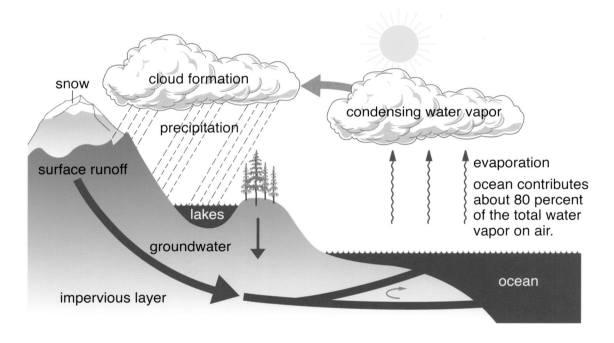

Figure 2

The water cycle

Want to Know More?

See appendix for Our Findings.

Further Reading

Math.com. "Surface Area Formulas," 2005. Available online. URL: http://www.math.com/tables/geometry/surfareas.htm. Accessed February 17, 2009. Formulas for finding the surface area of several shapes including a cube, rectangle, prism, and sphere are provided on this site.

Muse, M. R., and R. W. Hartel, "Ice Cream Structural Elements that Affect Melting Rate and Hardness." Originally published in *Journal of Dairy Science*, 2004. Available online. URL: http://jds.fass.org/cgi/reprint/87/1/1.pdf. Accessed February 17, 2009. This research paper, useful for the advanced student, shows a practical application of research on ice crystals in the manufacture of ice cream.

Worsley School Online. "Cooling With Ice," 2009. Available online. URL: http://www.worsleyschool.net/science/files/ice/andcooling.html. Accessed February 17, 2009. Prepared by teachers, this Web site explains how surface area affects the rate at which ice melts.

8. The Relationship of Temperature to Viscosity

Topic

The effects of temperature on the viscosity of oil can be determined in the laboratory.

Introduction

Automobiles engines are made of many metal parts that are constantly in motion (see Figure 1). The *friction* that occurs between moving metal parts can cause them to wear out very quickly. However, if the parts are lubricated, the wear is greatly reduced. Motor oil is used in automobiles to lubricate metal parts and reduce the friction. The oily coating also prevents the exposure of metal parts to oxygen, which can cause rust and corrosion.

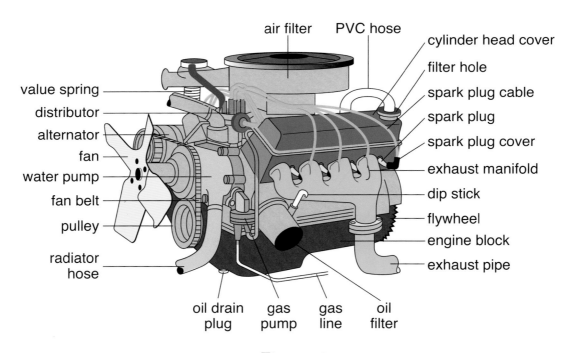

Figure 1

Automobile engine

Motor oils, which may be petroleum-based or synthetic, vary in thickness, or *viscosity*. The viscosity of oil refers to its ability to resist flowing or pouring. Highly viscous motor oils are thick and are able to coat well at high temperatures, whereas low-viscosity oils are thinner and will allow for efficient engine operation in cold weather. Many of the motor oils commonly used today have variable viscosity ratings and therefore have properties of thick and thin viscosity oils so that they can be used in a wide range of temperatures. In this experiment, you will test the viscosity of three variable-viscosity motor oils at different temperatures and determine which one is the thickest at each temperature.

Time Required

50 minutes

Materials

- 3 varieties of motor oil with different viscosity ratings
- 3 Celsius thermometers
- large hot plate
- hot mitts
- goggles
- 12 600-milliliter (ml) beakers
- marble
- wooden ruler
- stopwatch
- ice
- container for ice bath (cooler or plastic container that can hold 3 beakers)
- container for hot water bath (cooler or plastic container that can hold 3 beakers)
- graph paper
- access to the Internet
- science notebook

| Safety Note | Use caution when heating liquids on the hotplate. Wear goggles when working with chemicals. Take care when using the hot plate and when working with chemicals. Please review and follow the safety guidelines at the beginning of this volume. |

Procedure

1. Label the three oil containers as A, B, and C.
2. Label nine beakers as follows:

   A 0°C; A 25°C; A 70°C (for oil container A)
   B 0°C; B 25°C; B 70°C (for oil container B)
   C 0°C; C 25°C; C 70°C (for oil container C)

3. Fill each of the labeled beakers with 500 ml of the appropriate oil (A, B, or C).
4. Prepare an ice bath by placing ice and water in one of the containers. Place the three 0°C beakers in the ice bath.
5. The three 25°C beakers will remain on the lab table at room temperature.
6. Prepare a hot water bath by placing three beakers of water on the hot plate. Heat the water until it boils, then use hot mitts to pour the water in the other container. Place the three 70°C beakers in the hot water bath.
7. Monitor the temperature of all beakers and adjust water baths as necessary until the target temperature is reached.

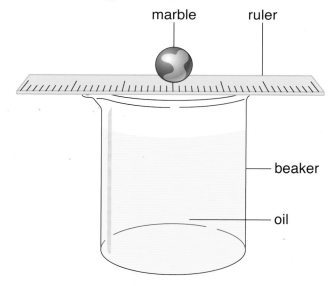

Figure 2

8. Lay a ruler across the top of one of the beakers. Place a marble on top of the ruler (see Figure 2).

9. Start a stopwatch at the moment that you push the marble off the edge of the ruler into the beaker of oil. Stop the stopwatch as soon as the marble hits the bottom of the beaker.

10. Record the amount of time it took for the marble to reach the bottom of the beaker in the appropriate column and row of the data table.

11. Remove the marble from the oil, clean it, and repeat in the same beaker. Record the second trial on the data table.

12. Repeat steps 9 through 11 with the remaining beakers, recording the times for two trials in each beaker.

13. Find the average of the times recorded for each of the two trials for each sample. Record the average time for each beaker on the data table.

14. Return the motor oil samples to their original containers and follow your teacher's instruction to dispose of them properly. Do not put motor oil in the trash or pour it down the sink.

Data Table				
Oil sample		Trial 1 time (sec)	Trial 2 time (sec)	Average time (sec)
Type A	0°C			
	25°C			
	70°C			
Type B	0°C			
	25°C			
	70°C			
Type C	0°C			
	25°C			
	70°C			

Analysis

1. Research the viscosity ratings of motor oil. Based on your findings, which type of motor oil tested in this experiment should have the highest viscosity at low temperatures? At high temperatures?

2. Did your experimental results agree with the expected results based on your research? Why or why not?

3. Create a line graph comparing the results of your experiment. Plot the average time required for the marble to fall at each temperature tested. Show the three different motor oils in different colors on the graph so that there will be three lines on the same graph, each with three plots representing the three temperatures.

4. How did the viscosity of motor oil change as it was heated?

5. When is it beneficial to use motor oil with low viscosity? When is it beneficial to use motor oil with high viscosity? Explain your reasoning.

6. Based on the results of your experiment, which type of motor oil would be the best to use in warm climates? In colder climates?

What's Going On?

Motor oil, like most other liquids, flows more easily when it is heated. However, unlike other liquids, motor oil needs to protect and lubricate at high temperatures. Thick oils are able to remain viscous at high temperatures, but may not flow freely in cold temperatures. To solve these problems, additives and polymers are introduced to motor oils, giving them variable viscosities.

Motor oils are rated to explain their formulation. The first number in the formulation is known as the "winter" rating and it measures the viscosity at near-freezing temperatures. The second number refers to the viscosity at high temperatures. Higher viscosity ratings indicate oil that is thicker at the specified temperature range. People select motor oils that suit their automobile type and that perform well in the climate in which they live.

Connections

Motor oil is used to lubricate metal parts within a combustion engine and prevent damage due to friction. Although motor oil is fairly efficient, it does not prevent all friction and corrosion. As an engine operates, some friction does occur between metal parts. This friction causes microscopic pieces of metal to be worn as metallic parts come in contact with each other. Over time, these metallic pieces accumulate in the oil, decreasing its efficiency and damaging the engine. For this reason, motor oil must be changed regularly. With routine oil changes, combustion engines can last for a very long time without the metal parts wearing out.

Want to Know More?

See appendix for Our Findings.

Further Reading

AA1Car. "Motor Oil Viscosity." Available online. URL: http://www.aa1car.com/library/oil_viscosity.htm. Accessed February 18, 2009. This Web site explains the oil viscosity rating system and discusses some special considerations for race cars.

HowStuffWorks. "What does the weight mean on a can of motor oil?" 2009. Available online. URL: http://auto.howstuffworks.com/question164.htm. Accessed February 18, 2009. This Web site explains the viscosity rating system used in describing motor oils.

Schappell, Kevin. "Oil/Lubrication," 2005. Autoeducation.com. Available online. URL: http://www.autoeducation.com/autoshop101/oil-change.htm. Accessed February 17, 2009. Schappell is a mechanical engineer who writes on a variety of topics related to cars.

9. Homemade Galvanometer

Topic

Galvanometers can be used to detect the flow of current through a circuit.

Introduction

A *galvanometer* is a type of *ammeter*, an instrument that is used to detect and measure small amounts of electric current. Galvanometers were first created in the 1820s, following the discovery by Danish scientist Hans Christian Ørsted (1777–1851) that the needle of a compass moves if the device is placed near an electric or magnetic field (see Figure 1). Italian physicist Luigi Galvani (1737–98), for whom galvanometers were named, is credited with the early use of devices to measure electric current. Since their creation, galvanometers have been used in many fields of science, engineering, and technology.

Figure 1

Reproduction of an early galvanometer

A basic galvanometer consists of a dial with a moving pointer that depicts the strength of the electrical current moving through wires of a circuit. In this experiment, you will create a galvanometer using a compass and insulated copper wire. You will then test your galvanometer and compare its accuracy to a commercial galvanometer.

Time Required

45 minutes

Materials

- compass
- 3 to 4 feet (ft) (91 to 122 centimeters [cm]), of thin insulated copper wire
- wire strippers
- electrical tape
- D cell battery
- D cell battery holder
- galvanometer
- science notebook

Safety Note   Use caution when working with electric currents. Be careful when using wire strippers and sharp metal wires. Adult supervision is recommended. Please review and follow the safety guidelines at the beginning of this volume.

Procedure

1. Tape the insulated wire to the back of the compass, about 6 to 8 inches (in.) (about 15 to 20 cm) from one end of the wire. Once taped in place, the wire will have a short end (about 6 to 8 in. [15 to 20 cm] long) and a long end.

2. Leaving the short end of the wire hanging freely, wrap the long end tightly around the compass until you have only about 6 to 8 in. [15 to 20 cm] remaining (see Figure 2). Make sure that you are still able to see the needle of the compass after wrapping the wire around it.

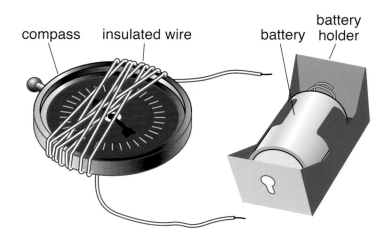

compass   insulated wire   battery   battery holder

Figure 2

3. Tape the coil of wire to the back of the compass to secure it.

4. Strip about 1 to 2 in. (2.5 to 5 cm) of insulation from each end of the piece of wire.

5. Place the D cell battery in the battery holder. Touch the two free wires to each of the battery terminals and watch the needle. Record your observations in your science notebook.

6. Switch the wires so that the one that was touching the "+" end of the battery is now touching the "−" side and vice versa. Record your observations in your science notebook.

7. Attach the ends of the battery to a commercial galvanometer and observe the results. Switch the wires, and see what happens. Record your observations in your science notebook.

Analysis

1. Why do you think the compass needle moved when the wires were connected to the battery?

2. A compass is designed to detect magnetic north. Based on the results of this experiment, what is the compass actually detecting?

3. Which way did the needle move when the compass was connected to the battery?

4. What happened to the compass needle after the battery was removed from the wires? Explain why you think this occurred.

5. What happened when the battery was connected to the commercial galvanometer?

6. How was the commercial galvanometer similar to the one created in this experiment? How was it different?

7. You tested the electric current from a battery in this experiment. What are some other possible uses for a galvanometer?

What's Going On?

A compass is a device that indicates north, south, east, and west, so it is used to find direction. The Earth has a core of molten metal, and therefore produces a magnetic field with two distinct poles (see Figure 3). A compass will align itself to magnetic north.

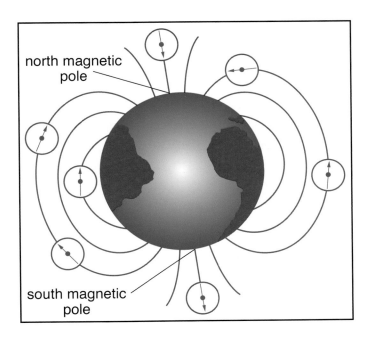

Figure 3

Earth's magnetic field

A magnetic field, like an electric current, is basically the flow of electrons from one area to another. A battery creates an electrical flow as electrons move from the "−" region to the "+" region. This movement is made possible when the two ends are connected by a conductive piece of wire. A galvanometer detects small electric currents in wires, such as those produced by a battery. The electrical current can be quantified by an actual galvanometer, which is used commercially to measure the strength of electric currents. The compass galvanometer made in this experiment is able to detect an electric current, and will even point in the direction of that electric current, but will not measure the strength of the current.

Connections

Electricity is essentially the movement of electrons that can be harnessed to do work within a system. Electrons are negatively charged and are thus attracted to positively charged particles. Within a battery, electrons tend to collect near the negative node and they flow through a wire toward the positively charged end. This is very similar to how a bar magnet operates. The flow of electrons causes one end of a bar magnet to have a "+" charge and the other to have a "−" charge. The particles within the magnet are polarized (charged) and they align so that their charges are all facing in the same direction. For this reason, a magnet is able to attract other metals that are easily polarized, such as iron.

Electromagnets are very strong magnets that are created by the flow of electricity through a piece of metal. They are similar to bar magnets in the sense that they also have two polarized ends. However, the strength of electromagnets can be varied depending on the amount of electricity flowing through them. They can also be turned off, unlike bar magnets. Electromagnets can be powered by batteries, or any other source of electricity, and are strong enough to move extremely heavy cars and other large metal objects.

 ## Want to Know More?

See appendix for Our Findings.

Further Reading

Clintberg, Byron. "Lesson 19: Galvanometers and Electric Motors." *StudyPhysics!*, August 5, 2008. Available online. URL: http://www. studyphysics.ca/index.html. Accessed February 19, 2009. Clintberg provides lessons on all basic physics concepts, including electricity and the use of galvanometers.

Nave, Carl. R. "Hyperphysics." Available online. URL: http://hyperphysics. phy-astr.gsu.edu/hbase/hph.html#hph. Accessed February 18, 2009.

Hosted by the Department of Physics at Georgia State University, Hyperphysics provides clear, concise information on all topics of physics, including electricity and magnetism.

Tatum, Malcolm. "What is a Galvanometer?" wiseGEEK, 2009. Available online. URL: http://www.wisegeek.com/what-is-a-galvanometer.htm. Accessed February 18, 2009. Tatum explains some of the uses of galvanometers.

10. Which Type of Food Contains the Most Energy?

Topic

A student-made calorimeter can be used to measure the amount of energy contained in snack foods.

Introduction

A *calorie* is a measurement of energy in the form of heat. You may be familiar with the term *calorie* as it pertains to food. The energy that is found in the food we eat is measured in nutritionist's calories. A nutritionist's calorie is an amount equal 1,000 calories, or 1 kilocalorie. Calories are an indication of the amount of energy our bodies can obtain from food. A typical adult requires about 2,000 calories of energy per day. Data Table 1 shows the types, number of servings, and examples of food in a 2,000-calorie-per-day diet.

Data Table 1		
Food group	**Servings**	**Examples**
Grains	6–8	1 slice bread 1 ounce (oz) dry cereal 1/2 cup (C) pasta or rice
Vegetables	4–5	1 C leafy vegetable 1/2 C vegetable 1/2 C vegetable juice
Fruits	4–5	1 medium fruit 1/4 C dried fruit 1/2 C fruit juice
Milk products	2–3	1 C yogurt 1 C milk 1/2 oz cheese
Lean meat, nuts, seeds, legumes	5	1 oz cooked meat, poultry, or fish 1 egg 1/3 C nuts 2 tablespoons (tbsp) peanut butter 1/2 C cooked dried peas or beans

The calories in food can be determined using a food *calorimeter,* a device that measures the amount of heat released as the food is burned. In this experiment, you will create a calorimeter and use it to determine the amount of energy in a variety of snack foods.

Time Required
90 minutes

Materials

- electronic balance
- coffee can
- soft drink can (empty and clean)
- glass stirring rod
- thermometer (Celsius)
- can opener (lever type)
- cork
- paper clip
- hot glue gun (with glue sticks)
- long-handled lighter or long safety matches
- tongs
- goggles
- graduated cylinder
- distilled water
- 4 snack foods to test (such as popcorn, chips, peanuts, marshmallows)
- science notebook

Safety Note Use caution when burning food items. Wear goggles at all times. Cans and water will become very hot. Use caution when using the hot glue gun. Adult supervision is recommended. Please review and follow the safety guidelines at the beginning of this volume.

Procedure

1. Answer Analysis questions 1 and 2.

2. Write the names of the four snack foods you plan to test in the first row of Data Table 2 beside the numbers 1, 2, 3, and 4.

3. Assemble the calorimeter using Figure 1 as a guide. To assemble:

   a. Use a can opener to make 2 small holes in the side of a soft drink can just under the top rim. The holes should be directly across from each other.

   b. Insert a glass stirring rod through the holes so that it can be used to suspend the soft drink can in the mouth of the coffee can.

   c. Straighten a paper clip. Insert one end of the paper clip into the smaller end of a cork.

   d. Glue the wide end of the cork onto the center of the bottom of the coffee can using hot glue.

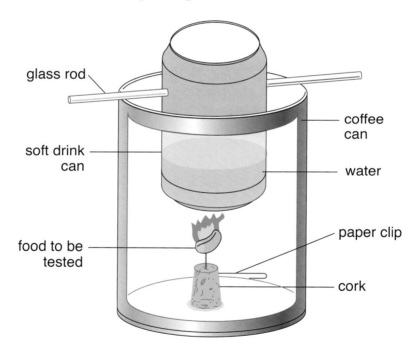

Figure 1

4. Measure 100 ml of distilled water in a graduated cylinder.

5. Place the soft drink can on the balance and press the zero or tare button. Pour the water into the soft drink can and find the mass. Record the mass of the water on Data Table 2 in the column labeled "1."

6. Place a thermometer in the mouth of the can and find the temperature of the water. Record the temperature on Data Table 2 as initial water temperature in Celsius (°C) in the column labeled "1."

7. Measure 2 or 3 grams (g) of food sample 1 on the electronic balance. Record the initial mass to two decimal places on Data Table 2 in the column labeled "1."

8. Attach the food sample to the free end of the paper clip at the bottom of the coffee can.

9. Using a long-handled lighter or long safety match, light the piece of food so that it burns. This may take a few tries.

10. Once the food sample is burning, immediately place the filled soft drink can over the burning food sample by resting the glass rod across the neck of the can.

11. Monitor the temperature of the water as the food is burning. On Data Table 2, in column "1," record the highest temperature reached.

12. Allow the apparatus to cool. Remove the soft drink can and pour out the water. Retrieve the remains of the burned food from the bottom of the can using tongs. Find the final mass of the remains of the food and record on Data Table 2.

13. Repeat steps 4 through 12 with the other three food samples, recording data in the appropriate columns of Data Table 2.

14. Answer Analysis questions 3 through 8.

Analysis

1. What were the four types of snack foods that you chose to analyze? Which one do you think will have the most calories?

2. Look on the nutrition labels of each of the foods that you chose. List the caloric content per serving for each food. Which one has the most calories? The least?

3. Calculate the mass burned of each of the food samples. To do so, subtract the final mass from the initial mass. Record the mass burned in the appropriate row of Data Table 2.

4. Calculate the temperature change of the water for each trial by subtracting the initial temperature from the final temperature. Record your calculations in the appropriate row of Data Table 2.

5. Plug the data from each column of the data table into the equation
   $Q = m \times C \times \Delta T$ where
   m = the mass of water used
   C = the specific heat of water, which is 1 cal/g°c
   ΔT = the change in the temperature of the water
      (final temperature − initial temperature)
   Show all work and record your answers for the Q values on the data
   table.

6. Determine the calories per gram for each sample of food by dividing
   the Q value by the mass of the food sample that was burned.

7. How did your answers compare to the calories per serving from the
   nutrition labels that you listed in Analysis question 2?

8. What are some sources of error that might account for differences
   in the nutritional and experimental values?

Data Table 2				
Food sample	1. _____	2. _____	3. _____	4. _____
Mass of water (g)				
Initial mass of food (g)				
Final mass of food (g)				
Mass burned (initial–final)				
Initial water temp (°C)				
Highest water temp (°C)				
Temp change (highest–initial)				
Q value (calories)				
Calories per gram				

What's Going On?

The calorie content of food indicates the amount of energy stored in that food. In your body, food is broken down slowly through a series of chemical reactions. The energy stored in the chemical bonds of food is harnessed to perform work for the body. As food is burned in a calorimeter, the stored energy is released as heat, and this heat causes the temperature of the water in the can to rise. Foods with high caloric content release more heat, and produce a greater increase in water temperature, than those of low caloric content. Generally, snack foods such as nuts contain the highest amount of energy per gram and baked snacks or foods like popcorn tend to have the least.

The biggest problem in *calorimetry* is that heat energy is lost easily as it radiates into the surrounding environment. Heat is a disorganized form of energy, and is difficult to contain and quantify because it constantly spreads out. Heat that is lost to the environment around the calorimeter system cannot be absorbed by the water in the calorimeter, and that energy is not measured and included in the calculations. The calorimeter created in this experiment is not insulated very well, and it loses heat easily. Actual calorimeters that are used to determine calories for nutrition labels are much more accurate than the one used in this experiment. They are more insulated and therefore less heat is lost to the surroundings and it can be measured more efficiently.

Connections

The calorie content of food is determined by the molecules that make up that food. Carbohydrates, fats, and proteins are food molecules that provide energy for body processes. Fats and oils are the most energy-rich food components. Foods that contain a high concentration of fats and oils have a lot of calories of energy per gram. Carbohydrates are the most energy-poor of the basic food components. Of course, foods are generally mixtures of the basic components as well as water, flavorings, spices, seasonings, vitamins, and minerals. These latter materials do not contribute any calories but can greatly alter the taste of foods.

Calories that are not used by the body for energy are stored as fat. If a person routinely takes in more calories than their body can use, obesity may result. As nutritionists learn more about the dangers of obesity, the food industry has responded by increasing its output of foods with low caloric values. These foods generally use a combination of flavorings, chemicals, and artificial sweeteners to imitate the taste of more calorie-rich foods.

Want to Know More?

See appendix for Our Findings.

Further Reading

Answers.com. "Calorimetry," 2009. Available online. URL: http://www.answers.com/topic/calorimetry. Accessed February 18, 2009. The Web site explains how calorimetry is used to find the caloric value of food.

Nutrition.gov. "What's in Food?" March 12, 2008. Available online. URL: http://www.nutrition.gov/nal_display/index.php?info_center=11&tax_level=1&tax_subject=388. Accessed February 18, 2009. This Web page discusses the nutritive value of carbohydrates, fats, and proteins as well as food additives.

University of Florida. "Calorimetry." Available online. URL: http://itl.chem.ufl.edu/2045/lectures/lec_9.html. Accessed February 18, 2009. In the lesson on this Web page, the formulas used in calorimetry calculations are explained.

11. The Heat Capacities of Zinc and Copper

Topic

Simple calorimeters can be used to determine and compare the specific heat of copper and zinc.

Introduction

Have you ever been burned by the metallic end of a car's seatbelt on a hot summer day? Metal objects heat up very quickly. Metals have very low *heat capacities*, or specific heats, the amount of heat energy, in *Joules* (J), required to raise one gram (g) of the substance by 1 degree Celsius (°C) (33.8 degrees Fahrenheit [°F]). A low specific heat is a desirable characteristic in materials that need to be conductive, such as pots and pans used for cooking.

The specific heat of a system can be determined using the equation for the energy in a system:

$$Q = m \, C_p \, \Delta T$$

where Q equals the total energy of a system, m equals the mass of the substance in grams, C_p is the specific heat of the substance, and ΔT stands for the temperature change in Celsius (final − initial). The first law of thermodynamics states that energy is not gained or lost in a reaction, it only changes forms. Therefore, the amount of energy gained by one part of a system must be equal to the amount lost by the other, and can be represented by

$$Q_1 = - \, Q_2$$

Knowing that the energies must be equivalent in a closed system, you can substitute the above equation with the following:

$$m_1 \, C_{p1} \, \Delta T_1 = - \, (m_2 \, C_{p2} \, \Delta T_2)$$

If the specific heat of one substance is known, you can use the above equation to determine the specific heat of the unknown substance by rearranging it as follows:

$$C_{p2} = m_1 \, C_{p1} \, \Delta T_1 / - (m_2 \, \Delta T_2)$$

In this experiment, you will build a calorimeter using Styrofoam™ coffee cups, then determine the specific heat capacities of copper and zinc samples based on the amount of heat transferred from the metals to the water in the calorimeter.

Time Required

90 minutes

Materials

- ➡ hot plate
- ➡ thermometer(s) (Celsius)
- ➡ beaker
- ➡ graduated cylinder
- ➡ 100 milliliters (ml) of distilled water
- ➡ access to tap water
- ➡ electronic balance
- ➡ piece of copper metal
- ➡ piece of zinc metal
- ➡ goggles
- ➡ tongs
- ➡ 2 Styrofoam™ cups (the same size)
- ➡ Styrofoam™ bowl
- ➡ science notebook

Safety Note   Wear safety goggles during this experiment. Be careful when using hot plates and heated glass, when working with water near electrical outlets, and when handling glass and thermometers. Please review and follow the safety guidelines at the beginning of this volume.

Procedure

1. Create a coffee cup calorimeter (see Figure 1). To do so:
   a. Take two Styrofoam™ coffee cups and stack them together to provide extra insulation.

b. Gently push a thermometer through the bottom of a Styrofoam™ bowl, creating a small hole. The Styrofoam™ bowl will act as a lid for the calorimeter, and the thermometer will be placed through the hole in the lid so that temperature readings can be taken.

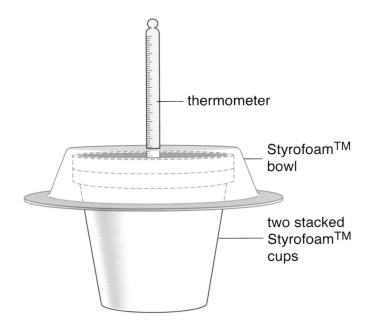

thermometer

Styrofoam™ bowl

two stacked Styrofoam™ cups

Figure 1

2. Use a graduated cylinder to measure 100 ml of distilled water.

3. Place the calorimeter base (the two cups) onto an electronic balance and press the "zero" or "tare" button. Add the 100 ml of water to the calorimeter. Record the mass of the water on Data Table 1.

4. Place the bowl lid (upside down Styrofoam™ bowl) on the top of the calorimeter. Use the thermometer to find the starting temperature of the water in the cups. Record the temperature on Data Table 1.

5. Fill a beaker (about 3/4 full) with tap water. The amount of water does not have to be exact. Place the beaker of water on the hot plate.

6. Find the mass of the piece of copper that will be tested. Record the mass on Data Table 1.

7. Carefully place the piece of metal into the beaker of water on the hot plate and allow the water to heat until boiling. Record the temperature of the water, which is the same as the temperature of the copper, on Data Table 1.

8. After 10 minutes, remove the piece of metal with tongs, quickly blot with a paper towel, and place it into the calorimeter. Carry out this step as quickly as possible so that the metal will not cool. Immediately place the Styrofoam™ bowl lid on the calorimeter.

9. Monitor the temperature of the water in the calorimeter. On Data Table 1, record the highest temperature reached by the water.

10. Repeat steps 2 through 9 with the sample of zinc. Record your findings on Data Table 2.

Data Table 1				
Mass of water (m_1)	Mass of copper (m_2)	Starting temp of water $(T_1$ water)	Starting temp of copper/water $(T_1$ copper)	Final temp of copper/water $(T_2$ copper/ T_2 water)

Data Table 2				
Mass of water (m_1)	Mass of zinc (m_2)	Starting temp of water $(T_1$ water)	Starting temp of zinc/water $(T_1$ copper)	Final temp of zinc/water $(T_2$ Zinc/ T_2 water)

Analysis

1. Calculate the temperature change (ΔT_1) of the water from the trial using copper by subtracting T_1, the starting temperature (before adding copper) from T_2, the final temperature (highest temperature reached after adding copper).

2. Calculate the temperature change (ΔT_2) of the copper by subtracting T_1 copper, the starting temperature (temperature of the boiling water) from T_2 copper, the final temperature (highest temperature reached by the water in the calorimeter).

3. Calculate the specific heat of copper (C_{p2}) using the appropriate values from the data table and from the calculations in Analysis questions 1 and 2 in this equation:

$$C_{p2} = m_1 \, C_{p1} \, \Delta T_1 / - (m_2 \, \Delta T_2)$$

The specific heat of water (C_{p1}) is 4.184 J/g °C.

4. Ask your teacher for the specific heat capacity of copper. How did your calculated value compare to the actual value? Calculate your percent error using the following equation:

   % error = (|actual value − experimental value| / actual value) x 100%.

5. Calculate the temperature change (ΔT_1) of the water from the trial involving zinc by subtracting the starting temperature (before adding zinc) from the final temperature (highest temperature reached after adding zinc).

6. Calculate the temperature change (ΔT_2) of the zinc by subtracting the starting temperature (temperature of the boiling water) from the final temperature (highest temperature reached by the water in the calorimeter).

7. Calculate the specific heat of zinc (C_{p2}) by plugging the appropriate values from Data Table 2 and from the calculations in Analysis questions 5 and 6 in this equation:

   $$C_{p2} = m_1 \, C_{p1} \, \Delta T_1 / - (m_2 \, \Delta T_2).$$

   The specific heat of water (C_{p1}) is 4.184 J/g°C.

8. Ask your teacher for the specific heat capacity of zinc. How did your calculated value compare to the actual value? Calculate your percent error using the equation

   % error = (|actual value − experimental value| / actual value) × 100%.

9. List some sources of error in this experiment that may have contributed to the percent errors in questions 4 and 8.

What's Going On?

When a metal sample was placed in boiling water, heat was transferred from the water to the metal so that it became the same temperature as the boiling water, approximately 100°C. When the metal sample was moved to the room temperature water in the calorimeter, the metal transferred heat to the water. The Styrofoam™ insulated the calorimeter, preventing most of the heat from escaping from the system. The amount of heat gained by the water is equivalent to the amount of heat lost by the metal. Assuming that no heat escaped to the surroundings, the specific heat of the metal can be calculated using the masses and temperature changes of the water and the metal, and the specific heat of the water.

The coffee cup calorimeter used in this experiment was not very efficient. Styrofoam™ is a good insulator, but it is not perfect. Additionally, some heat may have been lost through the hole in the top of the calorimeter where the thermometer was inserted or through cracks between the cups and the bowl lid. Aside from the inefficiency of the calorimeter, heat was likely lost to the environment during the transfer from the boiling water to the calorimeter. Scientists originally determined the actual specific heat values of these metals and others using multiple trials and a much more efficient calorimeter that did not require the metal to be transferred from one container to another.

Connections

Thermodynamics is the field of study concerned with the conversion of energy from heat to work. The first law of thermodynamics states that energy is never lost in a chemical reaction, but it may change forms. The second law states that the *entropy*, or disorder, of the universe is constantly increasing. The third law of thermodynamics tells us that the entropy of a solid at zero degrees *Kelvin* (K) is zero.

Heat and work are both forms of energy, and energy often changes between the two forms in chemical reactions. Although energy is not actually lost, it often moves into a less-organized form, which is not easily used. Heat energy easily diffuses into the surroundings of a system. Heat must be converted to a more ordered form to perform work in a chemical reaction. Chemical reactions that use heat from the surrounding environment to do work within a reaction are described as *endothermic*. Those that release heat to the surroundings are known as *exothermic reactions*.

 ## Want to Know More?

See appendix for Our Findings.

Further Reading

AUS-e-TUTE. "Heat Capacity Calculations." Available online. URL: http://www.ausetute.com.au/heatcapa.html. Accessed February 16, 2009. AUS-e-TUTE is an interactive science resource developed by teachers. This Web site provides a detailed explanation of the equations used in finding specific heat.

Blauch, David N. "Calorimetry: Specific Heat Capacity of Copper," Chemistry at Davidson, 2000. Available online. URL: http://www.chm.davidson.edu/ChemistryApplets/Calorimetry/SpecificHeatCapacityOfCopper.html. Accessed February 16, 2009. Blauch provides explanations and applets on various topics in chemistry, including specific heat.

De Leon, N. "Specific Heat and Heat Capacity," Chemistry 101 Class Notes, 2001. Available online. URL: http://www.iun.edu/~cpanhd/C101webnotes/index.html. Accessed February 15, 2009. De Leon's Web page offers simple explanations of several topics in physical science, including specific heat.

12. How Does LED Brightness Vary With Current?

Topic

Light-emitting diodes can be used to determine how light intensity is affected by the amount of current in a circuit.

Introduction

You most likely use multiple electronic devices every day. All electronic devices, from cell phones and MP3 players to computers, clocks, and digital cameras require an electric *current* in order to operate. Electric currents are produced by the flow of electrons from a source through a conductive material. The electron flow can be regulated and used to do work within a system. Batteries are used as a source of electron flow within a system. Electrons move from the negatively charged *anode* of a battery toward the positively charged *cathode*. Electric current travels very quickly; therefore, currents generally contain several *resistors* that slow the flow of electrons between the two electrodes of the battery.

Light-emitting diodes, or LEDs, are devices that convert electrical current into light. The color of light from an LED is determined by the type of metal within the diode. In this experiment, you will build several circuits and determine if the current flowing through the circuits affects the intensity of the LED light.

Time Required

60 minutes

Materials

- ➤ 3 AA batteries
- ➤ battery holder for 3 AA batteries
- ➤ red LED light (40–60 millicandles [mcd])
- ➤ 3 alligator clip leads

- five 1/4-watt resistors with different resistance ratings (ranging from 150–2,000 Ω)
- light meter
- tape
- opaque box or enclosure (large enough to cover the circuit and light meter)
- graph paper
- science notebook

Safety Note Use caution when working with electrical current, sharp wires, and breakable glass LEDs. Adult supervision is recommended. Please review and follow the safety guidelines at the beginning of this volume.

Procedure

1. Create a simple circuit like the one in Figure 1. To do so:

   a. Place 3 AA batteries in the battery holder.

   b. Use an alligator clip lead to connect the red wire of the battery (V) holder to the highest-rated resistor (R).

   c. Use another alligator clip lead to connect the resistor to the anode of the LED (the longer lead).

   d. Use a third alligator clip lead to connect the cathode of the LED (the shorter lead) to the black wire of the battery holder. Make sure that the two clips on the LED leads do not touch. You may have to bend the wires to prevent this.

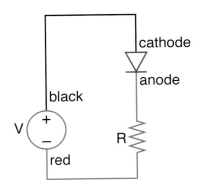

Figure 1

Simple LED circuit

2. Use the tape to attach the sensor of the light meter to the inside of an opaque box so that it faces toward the inside of the box. The display should be on the outside of the box so that you can read it easily.

3. Invert the box over the LED circuit and record the light output on the data table.

4. Repeat steps 1 through 3 with each of the five different resistors connected to the circuit.

Data Table	
Resistor strength (Ω)	Light intensity (lux)

Analysis

1. Was it necessary for all of the wires to be connected within the circuit before the LED would light? Why or why not?

2. What is the purpose of a resistor?

3. What might have happened if a resistor were not used in this circuit?

4. Create a line graph comparing the light output (Y-axis) to the resistor strength (X-axis). Connect all points with lines and be sure to label all parts of the graph.

5. How did the brightness of the LED compare to the strength of the resistor?

6. Did the current intensity within the circuit increase or decrease with the resistor rating? How do you know?

7. The current (*I*) traveling through a circuit can be determined using the equation *I* = *E/R*, where *E* is the voltage measured in volts (V) and *R* is the resistance measured in *ohms* (Ω). The voltage produced by three AA batteries is 4.5 V. Use the resistance ratings to determine the current (in amps) for each of the five trials.

What's Going On?

A resistor within an electrical circuit is made of a semiconductive material that slows the movement of electricity (charged particles) across its surface. The higher the rating of a resistor, the less conductive the material within it, and the less the flow of electricity. Resistors are very important in electrical devices because they restrict the flow of electricity, preventing too much from flowing from the source. If a LED were connected to a strong power source without a resistor, the strong electrical flow could damage the LED and drain the power from the batteries prematurely.

The force that enables electrons to flow between two regions is known as *voltage*, the amount of potential energy that is available in a circuit. The amount of current that actually flows through a circuit depends on both voltage and resistance within the circuit. The current flowing through a circuit is measured in *amps*, and the resistance is measured in ohms. The unit of resistance was named after Georg Simon Ohm (1789–1854), the German physist who discovered the connection between voltage (*E*), current (*I*) and resistance (*R*). According to Ohm's law, *I* = *E/R*. The Ohm's law equation can be rearranged in order to solve for any one of the three variables.

Connections

LEDs are commonly used in electronic devices because they fit easily into electric circuits and do not have filaments like those in typical lightbulbs that will burn out. Numeral displays on digital clocks, traffic lights, and on/off indicator lights on electronic devices are just a few of the products that contain LEDs. They are also used to transmit remote control signals to televisions.

LEDs contain a semiconductor chip at the center of their bulbs (see Figure 2). This chip has two regions, the *p region,* dominated by positive charges, and the *n region,* dominated by negative charges. There is a junction between the two regions of the semiconductor, and current will flow from the n to the p region when there is sufficient electric current. Once the current threshold is reached, the diode emits a specific wavelength of light. The type of semiconductive material determines the color of light emitted.

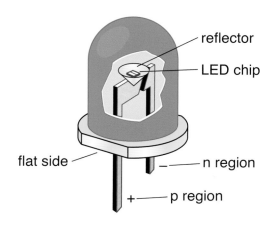

Figure 2

LED

Want to Know More?

See appendix for Our Findings.

Further Reading

All About Circuits. "How Voltage, Current, and Resistance Relate." Available online. URL: http://www.allaboutcircuits.com/vol_1/chpt_2/1. html. Accessed February 16, 2009. The authors provide simple diagrams and explanations of electric circuits.

Arnold, Rob. "How is LED brightness related to current?" LED Center, 2006. Available online. URL: http://led.linear1.org/how-is-led-brightness-related-to-current/. Accessed February 15, 2009. The relationship of LED brightness to current is explained on this Web page.

Physics Department, "Electricity Fundamentals," University of Oregon. Available online. URL: http://zebu.uoregon.edu/nsf/circuit.html#Ohm. Accessed February 17, 2009. Applets and diagrams on this Web page help explain Ohm's law.

13. Does Shape Affect a Ball's Energy?

Topic

The height of the bounce produced by a polymer ball can help determine how the shape of a ball affects its kinetic energy.

Introduction

Have you ever wondered why a ball like the one in Figure 1 bounces? Bouncing results from the transfer of energy between a ball and the surface that it contacts. When a ball is lifted up off the ground, it gains *potential energy*, energy due to position. The higher the ball is lifted, the more potential energy it contains. As the ball falls, it releases *kinetic energy*, the energy of motion. When the ball contacts a surface, it transfers some of its energy to the surface. If the surface is soft, such as carpet or a mattress, the energy is used to create an indention in the surface. If the surface is hard but the ball is flexible, only a small amount of energy is transferred to the surface, and most of the energy is reabsorbed into the ball, making it bounce. The more energy absorbed into the ball, the higher it will bounce. However, a ball will never bounce higher than the original position from which it was dropped because some of its energy is lost as heat due to friction and impact with the ground.

In this experiment, you will use a polymer made from sodium silicate mixed with ethyl alcohol to form several different shaped balls. You will drop the balls from a fixed height and determine which bounces the highest. From your data, you will be able to determine which shape is better able to reabsorb kinetic energy.

Time Required

60 minutes

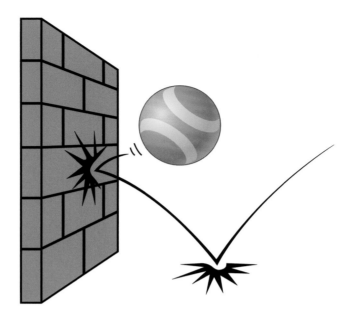

Figure 1

A ball bounces when it strikes a surface

Materials

- 20 milliliters (ml) of sodium silicate solution
- 10 ml of 95 percent ethyl alcohol
- 25-ml graduated cylinder
- 4 small disposable paper or plastic cups
- wooden splint or stirring rod
- butcher paper
- tape
- meterstick
- access to a sink with running water
- graph paper
- labeling pen
- goggles
- gloves
- access to the Internet or books on physical science
- science notebook

| Safety Note | Wear goggles when working with ethyl alcohol and other chemicals. Ethyl alcohol is very flammable; use caution when handling it. Do not handle the chemicals with your bare hands; wear gloves during the experiment. Please review and follow the safety guidelines at the beginning of this volume. |

Procedure

1. Pour 20 ml of sodium silicate solution into a small cup.
2. Pour 10 ml of 95 percent ethyl alcohol into the same cup.
3. Stir the solution with a splint or stirring rod until the mixture solidifies.
4. Put on a pair of gloves. Pour the solidified solution into your hand. Squeeze the solution over a sink so that the excess liquid is removed.
5. Form the solution into a shape of your choice. If the solution gets too dry, moisten slightly by placing it under running water for a few seconds.
6. Repeat steps 2 through 5 three more times, creating a different shaped ball each time. Label the balls as A, B, C, and D.
7. Answer Analysis questions 1 and 2.
8. Tape a sheet of butcher paper on the wall. Hold Ball A 100 centimeters (cm) (39 1/3 inches [in.]) off the ground near the lined paper on the wall. Drop the ball.
9. Have your lab partner mark the height of the first bounce made by the ball with a mark on the butcher paper.
10. Measure the distance from the mark on the paper to the floor. Record the distance on the data table.
11. Repeat steps 8 through 10 with each of the remaining rubber balls.
12. Answer Analysis questions 3 through 6.

Data Table				
	Ball A	Ball B	Ball C	Ball D
Height of first bounce (cm)				

Analysis

1. Sketch each of the four shapes that you created.

2. Research kinetic and potential energy. From what you find, predict which of the four balls will reabsorb the most kinetic energy and therefore bounce the highest.

3. Create a bar graph using the data that you collected, with the height of the bounce on the Y-axis and each ball along the X-axis.

4. Which of the shapes bounced the highest? The lowest?

5. Did the results of this test agree with your prediction in Analysis question 2? Explain why or why not.

6. Write a conclusion statement about the results of this experiment. Include a discussion of how the height of each ball's bounce is related to its shape due to the transfer of energy.

What's Going On?

The first law of thermodynamics states that energy is not created or destroyed, but is transferred into different forms. This law applies to the transfer of energy that takes place when a ball strikes the floor. Two factors influence the amount of energy transferred: the ball's mass and its surface area. The mass of a ball determines how fast it will *accelerate* toward the ground due to gravity. The acceleration of a ball will influence the force of its impact with the ground. For this reason, if a ball impacts the ground with enough force, it will cause an indentation to form in the ground, absorbing much of the energy from the falling ball. However, lightweight balls that are flexible and spring back into shape quickly will reabsorb the energy from the fall. Silicone is a lightweight and very flexible solid polymer that is capable of stretching and flexing, then returning to its original shape. Therefore, a silicone ball would bounce much better than a metal, glass, or plastic one.

The surface area of an object depends on its shape. The greater the surface area of a ball striking the floor, the great the transfer of energy from the ball to the floor. For this reason, a flat object, which has a relatively large surface area, transfers more energy to the floor than a curved object. Spheres have a very low surface-area-to-volume ratio. Therefore, the most efficient shape for a bouncing ball is generally spherical.

Connections

Many popular sports, including football, basketball, tennis, and soccer, involve balls (see Figure 2). Each of these sports requires balls that are lightweight and able to bounce efficiently. A ball, like one made from solid rubber, is heavy, giving it too much acceleration and force of impact for most sports. In a tennis match, a solid rubber ball would likely strain the arms of players on both sides of the net.

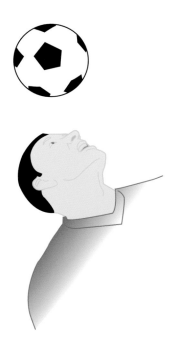

Figure 2

A soccer ball can be bounced off the head.

Hollow balls filled with air solve the problem. Air molecules move around freely. When a lot of air molecules are packed into a closed space, they simply compress and increase the amount of pressure within the object without adding much mass. Additionally, air molecules are not packed into any specific configuration; therefore, they are flexible and can spring back into shape easily. In order for a ball filled with air to bounce, it must contain enough air pressure to pack the air molecules in closely. If there is not enough air pressure, the ball may flatten upon impact with the ground. If this is the case, the kinetic energy found within the falling ball will be absorbed and change the ball's shape and, consequently, the ball will not bounce very high. Higher air pressure results in a more bouncy ball, which can be very important within the realm of sports.

 Want to Know More?

See appendix for Our Findings.

Further Reading

Bloomfield, Louis. "Bouncing Balls," HowEveryThingWorks.org, 2009. Available online. URL: http://howeverythingworks.org/bouncing_balls. html. Accessed February 15, 2009. On this Web site, Bloomfield answers students' questions about how and why things bounce.

Ophardt, Charles. "Silicon Polymers," Virtual ChemBook, 2003. Available online. URL: http://www.elmhurst.edu/~chm/vchembook/404silicone. html. Accessed February 15, 2009. Ophardt's Virtual ChemBook provides information on all topics of chemistry, including potential and kinetic energy.

Watson, David. "Energy Explained," FT Exploring, 2005. Available online. URL: http://www.ftexploring.com/energy/energy.html. Accessed February 15, 2009. Watson explains the first law of dynamics and related topics in an easy-to-read format.

14. Which Materials Are the Best Sound Insulators?

Topic

Different materials such as foam, air, paper, and wood have different sound-absorbing qualities.

Introduction

For you to hear a sound, sound waves must travel through a medium like the air and reach your ears. The ear is an organ that can channel sound waves and focus them on your eardrum, one of a series of structures that helps get information about the sound waves to your brain. Sound waves are *longitudinal waves* caused by the compression of particles in the air. As a sound is produced, it causes a disturbance in the air directly around an object. That disturbance pushes against adjacent molecules, creating areas of compression where particles are close together and areas of rarefraction where particles are widely space. These regions constitute the vibration of sound waves (see Figure 1). Sound waves move out from a central point (see Figure 2) much like water waves that ripple in all directions when a pebble is tossed into a pond.

We generally associate sound waves with air, but they can also travel through other types of mediums. In buildings, sound waves are capable of traveling through walls, which can sometimes be problematic. Often, people do not wish to be disturbed by loud noises coming from other rooms, so they will go to considerable effort and expense to install soundproofing materials. Soundproofing materials and techniques vary depending on the space and the type of sound involved. In this experiment, you will design a way to determine which common household materials provide the best sound insulation.

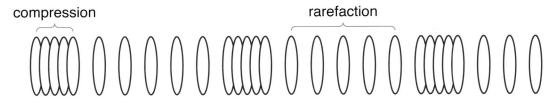

Figure 1
Structure of a sound wave

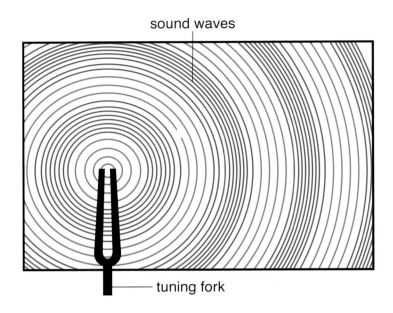

sound waves

tuning fork

Figure 2

A sound wave moves outward from its point of origin.

Time Required

60 minutes

Materials

- cardboard box (such as a large shoebox)
- small radio or MP3 player with speakers (that will fit easily inside box)
- cotton batting
- foam rubber
- small pieces of wood
- plastic zipper bags
- tissue paper
- aluminum foil
- ruler
- science notebook

> **Safety Note** Please review and follow the safety guidelines at the beginning of this volume.

Procedure

1. Your job is to design and perform an experiment to determine which materials make the best sound insulators.

2. You can use any of the supplies provided by your teacher, but you will not need to use all of them.

3. Before you conduct your experiment, decide exactly what you are going to do. Write the steps you plan to take (your experimental procedure) and the materials you plan to use (materials list) on the data table. Show your procedure and materials list to the teacher. If you get teacher approval, proceed with your experiment. If not, modify your work and show it to your teacher again.

4. Answer Analysis questions 1 through 3.

5. Once you have teacher approval, assemble the materials you need and begin your procedure.

6. Collect your results on a data table of your own design.

7. Answer Analysis questions 4 through 7.

Analysis

1. What properties do you think are important in a material used for soundproofing? Explain your thinking in two or three sentences.

2. Which materials do you think will allow the most sound to travel through them?

3. Write a hypothesis describing which of the materials available in this laboratory will provide the best soundproofing.

4. Describe the steps taken in your procedure in order to ensure that this was a controlled experiment. Why is this important to the accuracy of your experiment?

5. Which material provided the best soundproofing?

6. Which material provided the least sound insulation?

7. Did your results agree with your predictions? If not, what do you think may have caused the differences?

Data Table	
Your experimental procedure	
Your materials list	
Teacher's approval	

What's Going On?

The two basic types of soundproofing materials are sound absorbers and sound blockers. Materials that absorb sound are generally porous and provide a great deal of insulation. Foam, cotton, and clothlike materials are examples of sound absorbers. Thick absorptive materials convert sound waves into heat, which reduces or eliminates the progression of the sound wave. Musicians generally use absorptive soundproofing materials in their rehearsal studios or recording spaces because sound absorption prevents the sound waves from reverberating.

Thick, dense, nonporous materials may block sound waves. Heavy metals like lead prevent sound waves from traveling through them because of the absence of air. However, sound blocking materials cause sound waves to be reflected back into the space from which they were produced. A soundproofed room lined in nonporous materials may be quite noisy with echoes and reverberated sounds.

There are countless types of soundproofing materials used in homes and music studios. The type of material used ranges depending on function and personal preferences. Many materials use a combination of dense sound barriers and absorptive materials. The shape of the surface of soundproofing materials also determines their effectiveness. Many soundproofed walls have a rippled shape (see Figure 3) in order to increase the surface area and therefore the amount of sound turned into heat.

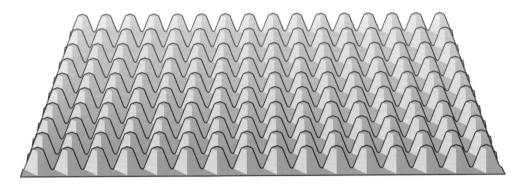

Figure 3

Soundproofing material

Connections

The speed at which sound travels in air refers to how fast the disturbance or vibration is passed from one air particle to the next. In other words, the speed of sound is the distance a sound wave covers in a specified amount of time. The speed of a sound wave in air depends primarily on two properties, pressure and temperature. Air pressure, the force exerted on you by the weight of the air, affects the density of air. At sea level, air pressure is about 14.7 pounds (lbs) per square inch (in.) (about 1 kilogram [kg] per square centimeter [cm]). Temperature of air refers to the heat content of air. The higher the temperature, the faster air particles interact with each other. At normal atmospheric pressure and a temperature of 68 degrees Fahrenheit (°F) (20 degrees Celsius [°C]), sound travels at about 750 miles/hour (mph) (343 meters/second [m/s]). To put this in perspective, normal highway speeds are much slower at 55 mph (24.6 m/s). On the other hand, light dramatically outpaces sound, traveling about 900,000 times faster.

Want to Know More?

See appendix for Our Findings.

Further Reading

Henderson, Tom. "Lesson 2: Sound Properties and Their Perception," The Physics Classroom, 2007. Available online. URL: http://www.glenbrook. k12.il.us/GBSSCI/PHYS/CLASS/sound/u11l2c.html. Accessed February 15, 2009. Henderson does an excellent job of explaining properties of sound and how sound travels.

MediaCollege.com. "How Sound Waves Work." Available online. URL: http://www.mediacollege.com/audio/01/sound-waves.html. Accessed February 15, 2009. Animations on the Web site help explain how sound waves travel through air.

Strickland, Jonathan. "Can Humans Hear in Space?" HowStuffWorks, 2009. Available online. URL: http://science.howstuffworks.com/humans-hear-in-space1.htm. Accessed February 15, 2009. Strickland discusses sound as a mechanical wave and explains how we perceive sound.

15. Materials That Interfere With Magnetic Energy

Topic

Some metals are able to interfere with magnetic fields.

Introduction

Have you ever wondered what makes magnets stick to your refrigerator? Magnetic attraction occurs between some materials because of the behavior of electrons within atoms. The core of an atom is composed of neutral neutrons and positive protons, giving the nucleus a positive charge. The electrons surrounding an atom's nucleus are negatively charged and are traveling around the nucleus. As each electron travels, it also spins (see Figure 1). In many metals, all of the electrons spin in the same direction, creating a *dipole*, an object that has two oppositely charged ends. Oppositely charged poles are attracted to each other while poles with the same charge repel. A bar magnet is an excellent example of a dipole (see Figure 2).

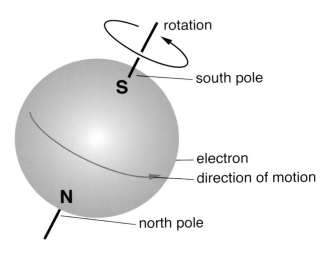

Figure 1

Magnetically charged objects have the ability to induce a dipole charge on other metal objects, causing them to have attractive and repulsive forces. This transfer of charges is what enables magnets to attract metal objects.

In this experiment, you will place a variety of objects between a metal paper clip and a bar magnet to determine which types of materials are able to block magnetic energy.

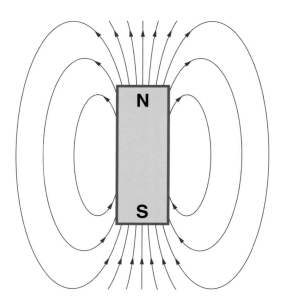

Figure 2

Magnetic fields of a bar magnet

Time Required

45 minutes

Materials

- strong magnet
- duct tape
- paper clip
- string about 12 inches (in.) (30 centimeters [cm]) long
- ruler
- scissors
- spring scale
- small piece of paper
- small piece of felt

- small piece of foam rubber
- small piece of plastic (about the thickness of milk jug plastic)
- small piece of wood (0.25 inch [in] thick) (0.6 centimeters [cm])
- small piece of aluminum foil
- small piece of steel (or cookware made of steel)
- small piece of iron (or cookware made of iron)
- small piece of copper (or cookware made of copper)
- science notebook

Safety Note   Please review and follow the safety guidelines at the beginning of this volume.

Procedure

1. Cut a piece of string that is about 12 in. (about 30 cm) long.
2. Tie one end of a string to a paper clip. Make a loop at the other end that you will be able to hook onto a spring scale.
3. Place the magnet on a flat surface such as a desk or countertop. Use duct tape to secure the magnet in place.
4. Hold the looped end of the string in front of the end of the magnet so that the paper clip is attracted to the end of the magnet.
5. Attach the spring scale to the looped end of the string and pull directly away from the magnet (parallel with the table). On the data table, record the force used, in newtons (N), to pull the paper clip away from the magnet.
6. Answer Analysis questions 1 and 2.
7. Place a piece of paper between the magnet and paper clip and repeat the spring scale test from step 5. Record the force used by the spring scale on the data table.
8. Repeat step 7 with felt, plastic, wood, foam rubber, aluminum foil, steel, iron, and copper. If the paper clip is not attracted to the magnet at all, record a "0" on the data table.
9. Answer Analysis questions 3 through 6.

Data Table	
Material used	**Force to remove paper clip (N)**
None	
Paper	
Felt	
Plastic	
Wood	
Foam rubber	
Aluminum foil	
Steel	
Iron	
Copper	

Analysis

1. Describe the attraction that occurred between the paper clip and magnet.

2. Which material do you think will be the most effective at interfering with the magnetic field between the magnet and the paper clip? Why do you think this is so?

3. Create a bar graph comparing the force used to remove the paper clip from the magnet for each of the different materials you placed between the magnet and paper clip in this experiment. Include the trial where no material was used.

4. Which material was the most effective at interfering with the magnetic field?

5. Which material was the least effective at interfering with the magnetic field?

6. From your data, what properties do you think enable a material to interfere with magnetic energy?

What's Going On?

Magnetic forces involve the movement of electrons within atoms. Each electron spins within a dipole, such as a bar magnet, and it aligns so that one end of the object has a "+" charge and the other end has a "−" charge. Each pole of a bar magnet affects the electrons in adjacent objects. If the nearby objects are metals, such as the paper clip used in this lab, the electrons also align. Oppositely charged areas of the dipole are attracted to each other. For this reason, metal objects such as a paper clip are attracted to any magnet or another metal that has a dipole.

Some material can reduce the magnetic force between two objects. Since all matter is composed of atoms, and those atoms can transfer energy and magnetic charges, magnetic forces cannot actually be blocked by any material. However, some materials that are easily magnetized are able to divert magnetic charges in different directions. An easily magnetized material, such as iron, can act as a shield against magnetic charges because it conducts the magnetic charge through itself instead of transferring it. This shielding effect is generally most effective if the shielding material is wrapped completely around the object that is to be protected from a magnetic charge.

Connections

Many devices such as computer chips, hard drives, and televisions involve very sensitive electronic parts. A strong magnetic field can realign their magnetic fields, causing changes that lead to serious problems with the devices. For this reason, engineers use a type of magnetic shielding to divert magnetic charges around sensitive materials within electronic devices. These shields are made out of very conductive materials such as iron or a specialized alloy known as *mu-metal*, a mixture of nickel, iron, and a small amount of molybdenum. Magnetic shields can be formatted to fit around an entire device or they can be fashioned so that they surround individual components within a device.

Magnetic shields work by redirecting the flow of magnetic charge so that it will flow around an object and not be transferred to it. When an object is magnetized, the dipoles align in specific arrangements known as field lines. As those charges are transferred from one object to another, the field lines are generally transferred in the same direction. However, an easily magnetized material, such as mu-metal, is capable of changing the direction of the field lines so that the magnetic energy can still flow, but it will be diverted around the object that is being shielded without damaging its configuration.

Want to Know More?

See appendix for Our Findings.

Further Reading

Alfieri, Catherine. "Physics." Available online. URL: http://www.mcwdn. org/Physics/PhysicsMain.html. Accessed February 16, 2009. Alfieri is a retired teacher who created this extensive virtual education Web site on physics and other topics.

PhysLink.com. "Ask The Experts," 2009. Available online. URL: http:// www.physlink.com/education/AskExperts/ae512.cfm. Accessed February 16, 2009. On this Web site, experts in various fields of physics discuss topics on magnetism and other areas.

Stern, David P., and Mauricio Peredo. "Magnetic Fields-History," The Exploration of the Earth's Magnetosphere, 2004. Available online. URL: http://www-istp.gsfc.nasa.gov/Education/whmfield.html. Accessed February 16, 2009. This extensive Web site provides information on specific topics in physics as well as an overview of topics related to Earth's magnetosphere.

16. Does the Diameter of a Speaking Tube Affect Volume?

Topic

Megaphones of different diameters produce sounds of varying volume.

Introduction

When your friends talk to you from across the room, you hear their voices because of the movement of sound waves. Sound waves are *longitudinal waves* produced by the compression of tiny particles in the air. When an object creates a sound, it produces vibrations in the air molecules directly around the object. Those air molecules then bump into adjacent molecules, compressing them. The energy of the compression moves outward from the source. To visualize a sound wave, think of a Slinky, a helix-shaped toy made of a loosely coiled metal spiral. Imagine stretching the toy between you and a partner. If you gather 10 coils in your hand, then release them, you can see a compression wave move from you toward your partner (see Figure 1).

Figure 1

A compression wave moves along a Slinky.

Unlike Slinky waves, which move in one direction only, sound waves radiate out in all directions from the point of origin. The movement of these waves can be channeled and amplified by certain devices. A simple way to amplify sound waves is by using a *megaphone*, a cone-shaped tube that projects voices for a great distance (Figure 2). In this experiment, you will create megaphones with different diameters and compare the effects they have on sounds.

Figure 2

A megaphone has one narrow end and one wide end.

Time Required

30 minutes

Materials

- poster board, 28 inches (in.) by 22 in. (about 71 centimeters [cm] by 56 cm)
- tape
- 12-inch ruler
- scissors
- tuning fork
- graph paper
- science notebook

Safety Note   Please review and follow the safety guidelines at the beginning of this volume.

Procedure

1. Cut a piece of poster board into four equal pieces.
2. Roll one of the pieces of poster board so that it creates a cone. Use the ruler to adjust the cone so that it has the dimensions (expressed in in.) of megaphone 1 on Data Table 1 and tape the side of the cone to hold the shape. Create the other three megaphones in the same way.

Data Table 1		
Megaphone	**Narrow end**	**Wide end**
1	2 in. (about 5 cm)	3 in. (about 8.5 cm)
2	2 in. (about 5 cm)	4 in. (about 10 cm)
3	2 in. (about 5 cm)	5 in. (about 12 cm)
4	2 in. (about 5 cm)	6 in. (about 15.25 cm)

3. Answer Analysis questions 1 through 4.

4. Strike a tuning fork on a solid surface, such as your desktop. Hold megaphone 1 so that the narrow end is 1 in. (about 2.5 cm) from the end of the tuning fork.

5. Have your lab partner place an ear 3 in. (about 7.5 cm) from the wide end of megaphone 1 and rate the volume of the sound heard on a scale of 1 to 10 (1 being very soft and 10 being very loud). Record the volume in Data Table 2.

6. Repeat steps 4 and 5 with the other three megaphones.

7. Answer Analysis questions 5 through 7.

Data Table 2	
Megaphone	**Volume**
1	
2	
3	
4	

Analysis

1. Draw a diagram depicting how the sound waves move from the tuning fork after it strikes the table top.

2. Draw a diagram depicting how you think the sound waves may look as they move through a megaphone.

3. Why do you think the megaphone changes the volume of the sound?

4. Which megaphone do you think will amplify the tuning fork sound most? Explain your reasoning.

5. Create a line graph with points depicting the relationship between megaphone diameter (X-axis) and the relative volume of the sound produced in them (Y-axis). Connect all points with lines and be sure to label all parts of the graph.

6. How is the diameter of a megaphone related to the volume of sound it produces?

7. Describe how the conical shape of a megaphone magnifies sounds.

What's Going On?

Sound waves carry energy. As they are produced, sound waves move in all directions from the point of origin. When sound waves hit a solid, they bounce off and resound through the air (Figure 3). The bouncing waves can either cause a sound to amplify or to *echo*, depending on its surroundings. If a sound hits a solid wall in an open area, it will generally bounce off and echo. However, if those sound waves are channeled through a narrow space, all of the energy travels in one direction and the sound is amplified.

When sound waves are focused through a megaphone, the cone-shaped device prevents the sound from moving in its typical circular motion. Inside the cone, sound waves bounce off the walls of the megaphone where they are intensified because the energy causing the wave to move is channeled into a smaller space. As the waves reach the wide end of the megaphone, they are spread out through a larger space. Therefore, in a megaphone, sound amplification increases with the circumference of the wide end, up to a point. If the wide end is too broad, the sound wave spreads out so much that sound amplification does not occur.

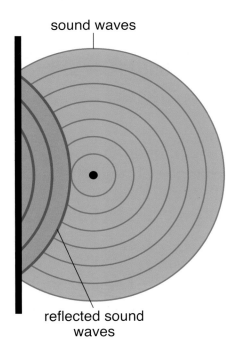

sound waves

reflected sound
waves

Figure 3

Sound waves are reflected when they strike a solid object.

Connections

Have you ever watched a science fiction movie that is set in outer space? Many of these movies depict battles or the movement of spacecrafts through open space with sound effects such as explosions. However, this is not an accurate representation of what would actually happen in space. Outer space is a *vacuum* and it does not contain air molecules. Since sound waves are compression waves that require the movement of air molecules, they cannot be transmitted in a vacuum.

Light waves travel in a different manner than sound waves. Light energy has a dual wave-particle nature. Light energy can act much like waves, but travels as particles known as *photons*. Thus, light does not depend on the existence of molecules for transmission. For this reason, the light from stars can travel billions of miles through space to your eyes here on Earth. Sound, however, cannot travel outside the atmosphere.

Want to Know More?

See appendix for Our Findings.

Further Reading

Megaphones. "A Loud Explanation of How Megaphones Work." Available online. URL: http://loudandclearmegaphones.com/A+Loud+Explanation+of+How+Megaphones+Work.3944.htm. Accessed February 20, 2009. This Web site explains the behavior of sound wave within the cones of megaphones.

Think Quest. "How Sound Moves," 2009. Available online. URL: http://library.thinkquest.org/C005705/English/sound/sound1.htm. Accessed February 19, 2009. Using simple explanations and diagrams, this Web site explains the behavior of sound waves.

TutorVista.com. "Wave Motion and Sound," 2008. Available online. URL: http://www.tutorvista.com/content/physics/physics-i/wave-motion-sound/wave-motion.php. Accessed February 20, 2009. An explanation of particle to particle wave transmission is provided on this Web site.

17. Comparing Densities of a Solid, Liquid, and Gas

Topic
Different states of matter display different densities.

Introduction
Matter, anything that takes up space and has mass, is all around you. All matter is made up of atoms, the basic fundamental units. Matter can undergo *physical changes* such as a change of state and retain their chemical integrity. The three most common states (phases) of matter are solid, liquid, and gas. Two less common states are *plasma* and *Bose-Einstein condensate* (BEC). Plasma is a highly energized state of matter made up of ionized gas. BEC is a state of matter that occurs within a degree of absolute zero. At this super-cool temperature, atoms begin to clump and they all take on the same qualities.

When matter changes states, it keeps the same atoms and molecules, but shows different physical properties like pressure, temperature, and density. A phase change can be brought on by an increase or decrease in the amount of energy present. For example, water can exist in the solid phase as ice. By adding energy in the form of heat, ice changes to water, which is in the liquid state. Further heating of water causes it to change into a gas, water vapor.

If you examined the molecules of ice, water, and water vapor, you would find that they are all the same: H_2O. But their physical properties differ. Physical properties include mass, color, shape, volume, and *density*. Mass refers to the amount of matter present and is related to the weight of matter. Volume is the amount of space that matter occupies. Density, the mass of a substance per unit volume, is a useful measurement because it is not dependent on how much of a sample you have. In this experiment, you will determine the density of matter in three phases.

Time Required
45 minutes

Materials

- small block of wood
- ruler
- graduated cylinder
- balloon
- bucket (that will hold the balloon when it is inflated)
- electronic balance
- waterproof marker
- access to water
- science notebook

Safety Note Please review and follow the safety guidelines at the beginning of this volume.

Procedure

1. Answer Analysis question 1.

2. Find the density of the solid block of wood. To do so:

   a. Measure the length, width, and height of the block in centimeters. To find the volume of the block use the formula

      $v = l \times w \times h$

      where l is length, w is width, and h is height. Record the volume in the appropriate section of Data Table 1.

   b. Use the electronic balance to find the mass of the block. Record the mass on Data Table 1.

   c. Calculate the density of the block of wood with the formula:

      $d = m/v$

      where d is density, m is mass, and v is volume. Record the density on Data Table 1.

3. Find the density of water. To do so:

   a. Use the graduated cylinder to measure 100 milliliter (ml) of water. Record the volume of the water on Data Table 1.

b. Use the electronic balance to find the mass of the water and the graduated cylinder. Record the mass in your science notebook. Pour out the water and dry the graduated cylinder. Find and record the mass of the empty graduated cylinder. Subtract the mass of the empty graduated cylinder from the mass of the cylinder and water to find the mass of the water. Record the mass of the water on Data Table 1.

c. Calculate the density of the water with the formula:

$d = m/v$

Record the density on Data Table 1.

4. Find the density of air. To do so:

a. Inflate the balloon, then tie the balloon to prevent the air from escaping.

b. Fill a bucket with water.

c. Use a waterproof pen to mark the level of water in the bucket.

d. Completely submerge the inflated balloon in the water (see Figure 1).

e. Use the waterproof pen to mark the level to which water rises in the bucket.

f. Remove the balloon and set it aside to dry.

g. Use a graduated cylinder to add water to the bucket until it reaches the level to which it rose when the balloon was submerged. The amount of water you added equals the volume of air in the balloon. Record the volume on Data Table 1.

h. Check to be sure that the balloon is completely dry. If not, pat it dry with paper towels.

i. Place the inflated balloon on the electronic balance to find the mass of the balloon and air. Record the mass in your science notebook. Pop the balloon, then place it on the electronic balance to find its mass. Record the mass in your science notebook. Subtract the mass of the popped balloon from the mass of the inflated balloon to find the mass of air. Record the mass on Data Table 1.

j. Calculate the density of the air with the formula:

$d = m/v$

Record the density on Data Table 1.

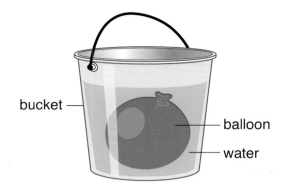

bucket
balloon
water

Figure 1

Data Table 1			
	Wood	**Water**	**Air**
Volume			
Mass			
Density			

Analysis

1. Which phase of matter do you expect to show the greatest density, solid, liquid, or gas? Explain your reasoning.

2. How do you find the volume of a solid?

3. How do you find the volume of a liquid?

4. Which of the three samples tested had the greatest density? The lowest?

5. Use the formula in the procedure to find the density of a block of aluminum that has a volume of 50 ml and a mass of 135 grams.

6. Describe an experiment in which you could compare the density of H_2O in the solid, liquid, and gaseous states.

What's Going On?

Density is a physical property unique to each element or compound. In a sense, *density* describes the relative heaviness of matter, which is due to how closely packed the atoms are. In Figure 2, which shows two boxes of the same volume, you can see that the box on the right is less dense than the box on the left.

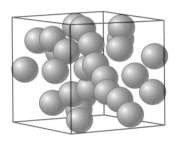 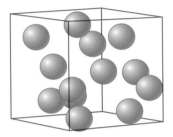

Figure 2

Two boxes of the same volume have different densities.

In this experiment, you compared the density of a solid (a piece of wood) to the density of liquid (water) and a gas (air). Generally, solids are denser than liquids, which are denser that gases. The experiment would have yielded different results if we had used ice as the solid. H_2O is one of the few compounds that is less dense as a solid than a liquid. You can easy see this when you put an ice cube in a glass of water. The ice floats rather than sinks. If you placed a cube of frozen alcohol in a glass of alcohol, it would quickly sink.

Connections

In chemistry, the density of materials is often compared to the density of water. This comparison is easily made when the material is placed in water to see if it floats or sinks. Anything that floats in water is less dense than water; objects that sink are more dense than water. The density of water is 1 gram/milliliter (g/ml). The densities of some other common materials are shown on Data Table 2. You can easily determine which substances will sink and which will float in water by examining this table.

The ability of an object to float is due to its *buoyant force*, a property related to density. However, you know that both wooden and metal boats

Data Table 2	
Substance	Density (g/ml)
Air	0.0013
Water	1.00
Ice	0.92
Wood	0.60 to 0.90
Aluminum	2.70
Silver	10.50
Gold	19.30

float, and metal is much denser than water. How can this discrepancy be explained? Boats made of metal contain many air-filled spaces. Ocean liners have cabins, dining rooms, and offices, all of which are filled with air. Air is much less dense than water, so the total density of an ocean liner is less than that of water.

Submarines are metal ships that regulate their position in water by varying their average density. Submarines have strong, double-walled hulls that contain ballast tanks, areas that can hold air, water, or a combination of the two (see Figure 3). When the ballast tanks are filled with air, the submarine's average density is less than that of water, so it can travel at the water's surface. To sink, the submarine replaces some of the air with water, increasing its mass and therefore its average density. Once the submarine is underwater, air is also pumped into the hull from compressed air tanks, giving the submarine neutral buoyancy and enabling it to hover. To dive, more water is taken into the ballast tanks.

Want to Know More?

See appendix for Our Findings.

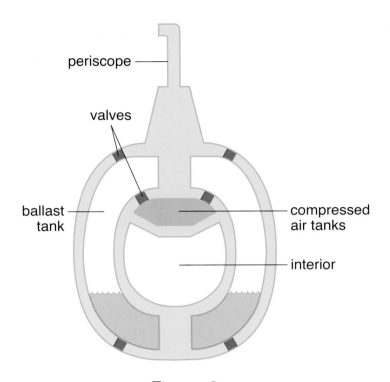

Figure 3

Cross section of a submarine

Further Reading

HowStuffWorks. "How Submarines Sink or Swim," 2009. Available online. URL: http://express.howstuffworks.com/express-submarine1.htm. Accessed March 1, 2009. This Web page explains how ballasts help submarines achieve neutral and negative buoyancy.

Kurtus, Ron. "Density of Matter," School for Champions, June 11, 2008. Available online. URL: http://www.school-for-champions.com/science/density.htm. Accessed March 1, 2009. Kurtus explains the basic concepts of the density of matter.

Pfaff, Raman. "Float or Sink, You Find Out," explorescience.com. Available online. URL: http://ww2.unime.it/weblab/mirror/ExplrSci/dswmedia/density.htm. Accessed March 1, 2009. On this interactive Web page, you can weigh objects, then put them in a beaker of water to see if they sink or float.

18. What Are the Best Friction-Reducing Lubricants?

Topic

An inclined plane and weighted sled can be used to compare the friction-reducing properties of various lubricants.

Introduction

Newton's first law of motion states that objects in motion will remain in motion until acted on by an outside force. However, if you roll a ball across the floor on a flat surface, it will eventually stop. Although nothing physically blocks the ball is motion, other forces are acting on it. The major culprit in slowing motion is *friction*, the force that resists motion due to contact between two surfaces. It is easy to understand friction between two rough surfaces because you can actually see and feel the bumps or ridges that come in contact with each other to resist motion. However, friction still occurs between objects that seem to be very smooth (see Figure 1). This is because at a microscopic level, the surfaces are still rough; this roughness causes the objects to rub together and lose momentum.

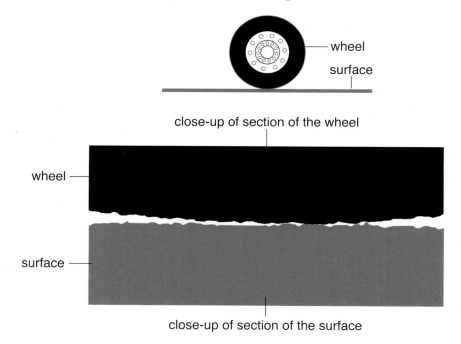

Figure 1

Friction exists between surfaces.

A *lubricant* is a substance that reduces the amount of friction that occurs between surfaces. Lubricants are often slippery materials that enable parts to move more freely across each other without wearing down their surfaces. Motor oil is a type of lubricant that enables engine parts to interact with little wear and tear. Lubricants can also reduce the amount of friction that exists between an inclined plane and an object sliding down the plane, thus increasing the speed of the slide. In this experiment, you will test several different lubricants to determine which is the most effective at reducing friction.

Time Required

45 minutes

Materials

- smooth board (at least 14 inches [in.] long and 4 in. wide) (35.6 centimeters [cm] long and 10.2 cm wide)
- block or brick (about 6 in. [15.2 cm] tall)
- aluminum sheet (the same length as the smooth board)
- protractor
- duct tape
- small wooden block (or other flat object to slide down inclined plane)
- vegetable oil
- baby oil
- mineral oil
- petroleum jelly
- liquid soap
- 25-milliliter (ml) beaker
- paper towels
- rubbing alcohol
- soap
- stopwatch

- graph paper
- access to water
- science notebook

Safety Note   **Please review and follow the safety guidelines at the beginning of this volume.**

Procedure

1. Work with a lab partner.

2. Observe the physical characteristics (such as thickness, color, how slippery they feel) of the five lubricants (vegetable oil, baby oil, mineral oil, petroleum jelly, and liquid soap). Record your observations on the data table. Answer Analysis questions 1 and 2.

3. Create an inclined plane (a ramp) with an incline between 45 degrees and 65 degrees by propping a smooth board on a block or brick. Place your ramp on a flat surface, such as a table or the floor. Measure the angle of the incline using a protractor and record it in your science notebook. You will need to ensure that the incline is constant for all trials of the experiment.

4. Place an aluminum sheet on the inclined plane surface. Secure it with strong tape if needed. (Be sure that the tape is placed in a location where it will not interfere with an object sliding down the ramp).

5. Place a small wooden block or object with a flat edge at the top of the inclined plane (see Figure 2). Have your partner start the stopwatch at the instant that you release the block and stop the stopwatch when it hits the floor or table at the bottom of the ramp. Record the time on the data table in the row labeled "no lubricant."

6. Measure 15 ml of one of the lubricants in the graduated cylinder. Spread the lubricant evenly onto the aluminum surface.

7. Place the block at the top of the inclined plane. Begin the stopwatch when the block is released and stop it when the block reaches the end of the ramp. Record the time it takes for the block to slide down the ramp in the appropriate row of your data table.

8. Clean the aluminum sheet, block, and graduated cylinder with soap, water, and paper towels. Wipe all surfaces with rubbing alcohol to remove any residue.

9.   Repeat steps 6 through 8 with each lubricant.

10. Answer Analysis questions 3 through 6.

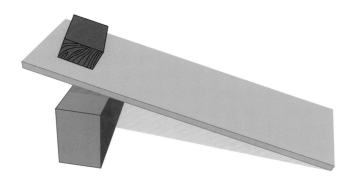

Figure 2

Block sliding down inclined plane.

Data Table		
Lubricant	**Observations**	**Time for object to slide**
No lubricant	N/A	
Vegetable oil		
Baby oil		
Mineral oil		
Petroleum jelly		
Liquid soap		

Analysis

1.   Which lubricant do you think will best reduce the friction between the block and the ramp? Which lubricant do you think will be least effective at reducing friction between the block and ramp?

2. Justify your answers to Analysis question 1 based on the observations that you made about each of the lubricants.

3. Create a bar graph showing the time it took for the block to slide down the ramp in each trial. Be sure to label all parts of the graph.

4. Which lubricant enabled the block to slide the fastest?

5. What property of the "best" lubricant do you think was the most important factor in reducing the friction between the block and ramp?

6. Given that one of the lubricants that you used worked best at reducing friction in this test, why do you think there are so many different types of lubricants available?

What's Going On?

Although a block of wood and a sheet of aluminum both appear to have smooth surfaces, friction still occurs between them. Even when surfaces feel smooth, they still have texture on a microscopic level. These microscopic bumps and ridges generate heat when they rub together and slow the movement of an object. When a block slides down a ramp, it moves downward due to the pull of gravity; but its downward acceleration is slowed due to the friction between the block and the ramp. Adding lubricants can reduce the friction that occurs between two surfaces.

Lubricants come in many forms; they can be liquid or solid, natural or synthetic. The type of lubricant used depends on the situation. For instance, motor oil in a car engine has to resist friction at high engine temperatures, yet be thin enough to allow free movement of engine parts when they are cold. Silicone or petroleum jellies are often used in plumbing to allow tight-fitting pipe joints to join easily. Biomedical lubricants are used to prevent damage to bones in joints like the knee and elbow. When it comes to lubricating a ramp, thinner, oily lubricants will tend to be more effective than thicker solid ones. This is because solid lubricants often interfere with the downward motion that is occurring.

Connections

Is friction a friend or foe? The answer to this question is, "It depends." If you are trying to slide a heavy box up an inclined plane (a ramp), friction makes the work difficult. But when you are driving your car, you want some friction between the tires and the road to prevent sliding. The tires on cars, trucks, and buses are designed to have a high *coefficient of friction*, with a dry highway surface. The coefficient of friction is the ratio of the force it takes to slide two surfaces across each other to the force that is pressing those forces together. The higher the coefficient of friction, the less likely it is that two surfaces will slide across each other. Because there is plenty of friction between the tire and road, cars stay on the road and out of the ditch. However, ice causes problems. When a car on ice applies the brakes, the heat generated by the sliding tires melts the top layer of ice and changes it to water. The ice acts like a lubricant, dramatically reducing the coefficient of friction between tires and roadway, so skidding occurs. Once a car begins to skid, it will continue to do so until something applies an equal and opposite force to end the motion. That "something" is often another car, an embankment, or a telephone pole.

Want to Know More?

See appendix for Our Findings.

Further Reading

Department of Physics and Astronomy. "Newton's Three Laws of Motion," University of Texas, 2009. Available online. URL: http://csep10.phys. utk.edu/astr161/lect/history/newton3laws.html. Accessed February 23, 2009. This Web site states and briefly explains Newton's ideas on forces and motion.

Taylor, Ian. "Fact or Friction," physicsworld.com, February 4, 2002. Available online. URL: http://physicsworld.com/cws/article/print/5020. Accessed February 23, 2009. Taylor discusses friction, car engines, and the types of lubricants needed in motor vehicles.

University of Washington. "Introduction to Tribology—Friction." Available online. URL: http://depts.washington.edu/nanolab/ChemE554/ Summaries%20ChemE%20554/Introduction%20Tribology.htm. Accessed February 23, 2009. Written for the advanced student, this Web page explains the history of tribology, a field of science that works with lubricants.

19. Arrow Mass and Depth of Penetration

Topic

The mass of an arrow affects the depth of that arrow's penetration.

Introduction

Archery, an activity that predates written history, involves the use of a bow to launch a *projectile*, the arrow. Archery was originally a tool used in hunting and warfare. Although some hunters still prefer a bow and arrow, archery has also evolved into a sport of precision where archers aim at targets and compete on their accuracy.

An arrow has four basic parts (see Figure 1). The tip or point of the arrow, the arrowhead, is mounted on a shaft. Many different arrow points are available, depending on their purpose. The long spine or shaft of an arrow can be made from wood, aluminum, or fiberglass. The arrow's fletching, real or synthetic feathers on the shaft, give the arrow stability as it flies through the air. The notching is the point where the arrow fits into the bow string.

arrowhead or tip

fletching

shaft

fletching   notching

Figure 1

Parts of an arrow

The size, mass, and shape of the arrow and point are important for accuracy of shooting. The depth to which an arrow penetrates its target is affected by the mass of the arrow tip. Arrow tip mass is measured in *grains* (gr), a British unit that is much smaller than a gram (g). In this experiment, you will shoot arrows with tips of different masses at a target and determine the effect that mass has on the depth of arrow penetration.

110

Time Required

60 minutes

Materials

- ⚬ access to an outdoor area
- ⚬ bow
- ⚬ arrow
- ⚬ armguard
- ⚬ goggles
- ⚬ 3 arrow tips with different masses (85 gr, 100 gr, and 125 gr)
- ⚬ target (at least 18 inches [46 centimeters] thick)
- ⚬ target stand
- ⚬ markers or marking pens in several colors
- ⚬ ruler
- ⚬ tape measure
- ⚬ masking tape
- ⚬ science notebook

Safety Note Be sure to shoot arrows in a location away from houses, cars, people, animals, or any other valuable objects. Never aim the arrows at any person or object other than the target. Never attempt to shoot damaged or broken arrows. Wear goggles and an armguard when using the bow and arrow. Please review and follow the safety guidelines at the beginning of this volume.

Procedure

1. Answer Analysis question 1.
2. Set up your target on a stand in a field or other open area.
3. Use a tape measure to mark a shooting line 75 feet (ft) (23 meters [m]) from the target. Create a line on the ground using masking tape.

4. While standing on the line, take several practice shots using the bow and arrows until you gain a comfortable amount of precision.

5. Use a marking pen, draw a line on the shaft of arrow indicating the point to which you will draw the arrow back for each shot.

6. Place the lightest (85 gr) tip on the arrow.

7. While standing on the shooting line, draw the arrow back to the mark that you created and shoot at the target.

8. On the arrow, mark the depth of penetration on the shaft. Remove the arrow and measure the distance from the mark to the tip of the arrow. Record this distance on the data table.

9. Repeat the steps 7 through 8 three more times with this arrow tip.

10. Find the average depth of penetration for this arrow tip and record it on the Data Table.

11. Repeat steps 7 through 10, using the two other arrow tips.

12. Answer Analysis questions 2 through 6.

Data Table					
Arrow tip	Trial 1 depth	Trial 2 depth	Trial 3 depth	Trial 4 depth	Average
85 gr					
100 gr					
125 gr					

Analysis

1. Write a hypothesis stating what effect you think the mass of an arrow will have on its depth of penetration. Explain the reasoning behind your hypothesis.

2. Describe the factors that you held constant in this experiment. Why is it important to keep these factors constant?

3. Which arrow penetrated the deepest into the target?

4. Was your hypothesis correct? If not, explain why you think this was so.

5.   Write a statement explaining the effect on an arrow's mass on its depth of penetration.

6.   What were some possible sources of error in this experiment?

What's Going On?

The mass of an arrow affects its speed and the depth of its penetration into a target. When selecting an arrow tip, an archer must keep in mind that a heavy tip penetrates deeper into a target because it builds up a greater velocity by the time it reaches its intended target. However, a lightweight, smaller arrow tip travels faster. A faster arrow is able to arrive at its target more quickly, and because there is less effect from the pull of gravity, the arrow often reaches its target with more accuracy.

The mass of an arrow tip chosen by an archer depends on the purpose for which it was intended, much like the shape and size of the arrow itself. An archer who is aiming at a target will likely choose a very light aerodynamic arrow tip to ensure the speed and accuracy of the shot. A hunter who is interested in a quick kill, however, may choose a heavier arrow tip which will penetrate deeper into the animal and be much more effective. Of course, a very heavy arrow tip will cause the arrow to be slower and some accuracy will be sacrificed.

Connections

An arrow is a type of projectile, an object that is projected through the air at an angle. Other projectiles include balls, bullets, cannonballs, and rockets. When a projectile is traveling toward a target, it does not travel in a straight line from the point of its release. Instead, it takes an arclike path, which eventually leads to the ground. Figure 2 shows the path of a cannonball after it is shot from a cannon. The arc is caused by a combination of gravity, which pulls the cannonball down toward the Earth, and the force from the cannon, which propels it forward.

The arclike trajectory of projectiles must be considered by an archer when aiming for a target. To hit the target, an archer aims slightly higher than the bulls-eye. The heavier the arrow tip, the more an archer must adjust his or her aim because heavy objects are affected more by gravity than light ones. In addition, a heavy object thrown or shot using a certain amount of force cannot travel as far as a light object propelled by the same amount of force. The heavy object would begin to arc earlier and fall toward the ground sooner than a light one.

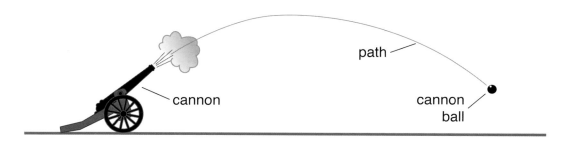

Figure 2
Projectile motion

Want to Know More?

See appendix for Our Findings.

Further Reading

Ashby, Ed. "Arrow Lethality Study Update—2005," 2006. Available online. URL: http://www.alaskabowhunting.com/PR/Ashby_2005_Update_6.pdf. Accessed February 24, 2009. While explaining the penetration of heavy bone, Ashby provides insight into how mass affects arrow penetration.

Hunter's Friend. "Arrow Buyer Help: Arrow Length and Mass Considerations," 2008. Available online. URL: http://www.huntersfriend. com/2007-Carbon-Arrows/arrow-selection-guide2.htm. Accessed on February 24, 2009. This Web site explains arrow specifications for hunters, including arrow weight.

School of Physics and Astronomy. "Projectile Motion," University of Minnesota. June 25, 2007. Available online. URL: http://www.physics. umn.edu/outreach/pforce/circus/projectile.html. Accessed February 24, 2009. The effect of gravity on projectile motion is briefly discussed on this Web site.

20. Variables That Affect Speed

Topic

Variables that affect the speed of a metal ball rolling down a ramp can be determined in student-designed experiments.

Introduction

When you first learned to ride a bike, you quickly found out that you travel faster down a hill than you do on flat ground (see Figure 1). The *speed* that you reached on your downhill rides depended on your weight, the length of the hill, and the steepness of the hill. Speed is the amount of distance covered within a certain period of time.

Figure 1

Bikes reach greater speeds on steep slopes than on level ground.

You can understand the behavior or bicycles on a hill by experimenting with a ball that rolls down an *inclined plane* or ramp. When a ball rolls down a ramp, it experiences *acceleration*, or change in speed. Many different factors influence the acceleration of an object rolling down a ramp, including the object's mass and distribution, the *slope* of the ramp, the length of the ramp, and the friction between the ball and ramp. In this experiment, you will develop a hypothesis predicting how one factor affects the ball's speed, then design and perform an experiment to test your hypothesis.

Time Required

45 minutes

Materials

- assorted metal balls with different diameters
- plastic track material
- piece of wood (2 inches [in.] x 4 in.) (5.1 centimeters (cm) by 10.2 cm)
- hammer
- nails
- scissors
- cement block
- tape
- electronic balance
- protractor
- stopwatch
- meterstick
- science notebook

Safety Note   Use extreme caution when using hammer and nails if your procedure calls for them. Please review and follow the safety guidelines at the beginning of this volume.

Procedure

1. Your job is to design and perform an experiment to find out how one *variable* affects the speed of a ball rolling down a ramp. Variables that you can test include diameter of the ball, mass of the ball, slope of the ramp, length of the ramp, and friction between the ramp and the ball.

2. You can use any of the supplies provided by your teacher, but you may not need to use all of them.

3. Before you conduct your experiment, decide exactly what you are going to do. Write the steps you plan to take (your experimental procedure) and the materials you plan to use (materials list) on the data table. As you are planning your experiment, keep these points in mind:

   a. In your experiment, control for all of the variables except the one you are testing.

   b. Before you begin, decide what data you want to collect.

4. Show your procedure and materials list to the teacher. If you get teacher approval, proceed with your experiment. If not, modify your work and show it to your teacher again.

5. Answer Analysis questions 1 and 2.

6. Once you have teacher approval, assemble the materials you need and begin your procedure.

7. Collect your results on a data table of your own design.

8. Answer Analysis questions 3 thorugh 5.

Analysis

1. Write a hypothesis stating how the variable you will test will affect the speed of a ball rolling down a ramp. Justify your thinking.

2. What steps did you include in your procedure to ensure that it was a controlled test?

3. Why is it important not to change more than one variable at a time in a controlled experiment?

4. List some sources of error in this experiment. How do you think these may have affected your final outcome?

5. If you were going to do this experiment again, what changes would you make to improve it?

Data Table	
Your experimental procedure	
Your materials list	
Teacher's approval	

What's Going On?

Both bicycles and balls rolling down inclined planes experience *forces*, pushes or pulls. A force has two components: size and direction. Forces acting on objects include the pull of gravity (weight of the object), the supporting force (in this case, the ramp), and friction, which opposes the motion (see Figure 2). The sum of all the forces acting on an object is the *net force*. If forces are unbalanced, they will cause a change in motion (acceleration) or a change in the direction of the motion.

When a ball rolls down a ramp, it accelerates as it rolls. The more it accelerates, the faster the ball will be moving when it comes to the end of the ramp (and the faster it will get to the end of the ramp). A ball will accelerate more if it is on a steeper ramp, or if it is heavier because the downward force is increased, which will increase the acceleration of the ball. Additionally, if a ball rolls down a longer ramp, it has more time to accelerate and will therefore gain more speed before it reaches the end of the ramp.

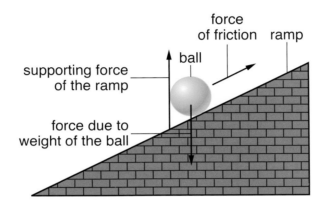

Figure 2

Forces acting on a rolling ball

The acceleration of a ball depends greatly on the distribution of its mass away from a central axis. Because of this, if two balls have the same mass but different radii, the smaller ball will accelerate faster. Likewise, if two balls have the same radius but different masses, the more massive ball will win. This is because in a large lightweight ball, more mass is distributed away from the central axis of rotation; therefore, it has a larger moment of inertia and is less likely to accelerate.

Connections

If you roll a tennis ball and a bowling ball down the same ramp, which one will go faster? The bowling ball will go faster because of its mass. However, if you were to drop the same two balls from the same height (with no wind resistance), they would reach the ground at the exact same time. When an object is falling freely, it always accelerates at the same rate, regardless of its mass. This is because of gravity. Whatever the mass of an object, it will always fall to the ground at an acceleration of 9.8 meters per second (m/sec) squared (32 feet per second [ft/sec] squared). The only reason that some lightweight objects may fall more slowly than heavier ones is because they are more affected by wind resistance. Therefore, in a vacuum, where there are no air molecules, a feather and a grand piano released from the same location would hit the ground at the exact same time.

Want to Know More?

See appendix for Our Findings.

Further Reading

Fowler, Michael. "Galileo's Acceleration Experiment." Available online. URL: http://galileoandeinstein.physics.virginia.edu/lectures/gal_accn96.htm. Accessed March 1, 2009. Fowler, of the University of Virginia Physics Department, explains the work of Galileo on the behavior of falling and rolling objects.

Stanbrough, J. L. "Falling, Sliding, and Rolling," April 21, 2008. Available online. URL: http://www.batesville.k12.in.us/physics/PhyNet/Mechanics/RotMechanics/fall_slide_roll.htm. Accessed March 1, 2009. Stanbrough explains the forces that act on masses rolling or sliding down inclined planes.

Teacher Tube. "Ball Rolling Down a Ramp," 2009. Available online. URL: http://www.teachertube.com/view_video.php?viewkey=5961172274194b3525c1. Accessed March 1, 2009. Teacher Tube is an online community for sharing instructional videos. On this site, a teacher explains how to determine the velocity of a ball rolling down a ramp.

Scope and Sequence Chart

This chart aligns the experiments in this book with some of the National Science Content Standards. (These experiments do not address every national science standard.) Please refer to your local and state content standards for additional information. As always, adult supervision is recommended and discretion should be used in selecting experiments appropriate to each age group or to individual students.

Standard	Grades 5–8	Grades 9–12
Physical Science		
Properties and changes of properties in matter	1, 4, 6, 7, 8, 11, 17	1, 4, 6, 7, 8, 11, 17
Chemical reactions	1, 5, 6, 10, 13	1, 5, 6, 10, 13
Motions and forces	2, 8, 13, 18, 19, 20	2, 8, 13, 18, 19, 20
Transfer of energy and interactions of energy and matter	2, 3, 5, 9, 10, 11, 12, 13, 14, 15, 16	2, 3, 5, 9, 10, 11, 12, 13, 14, 15, 16
Conservation of energy and increase in disorder	11, 13	11, 13
Life Science		
Cells and structure and function in living systems	1	1
Reproduction and heredity		
Regulation and behavior		

Standard	Grades 5–8	Grades 9–12
Populations and ecosystems		
Diversity and adaptations of organisms		
Interdependence of organisms		
Matter, energy, and organization in living systems		
Biological evolution		
Earth Science		
Structure and energy in the Earth system		
Geochemical cycles	4, 7	4, 7
Origin and evolution of the Earth system		
Origin and evolution of the universe		
Earth in the solar system	2, 3	2, 3
Nature of Science		
Science in history	2, 4, 9, 12	2, 4, 9, 12
Science as an endeavor	all	all

Grade Level

Setting

The experiments are classified by materials and equipment use as follows:

- Those under SCHOOL LABORATORY involve materials and equipment found only in science laboratories. Those under SCHOOL LABORATORY must be carried out there under the supervision of the teacher or another adult.

- Those under HOME involve household or everyday materials. Some of these can be done at home, but call for supervision.

- The experiments classified under OUTDOORS may be done at the school or at the home, but call for supervision.

SCHOOL LABORATORY

1. Accuracy of Labeling Vitamin C in Orange Juice
7. The Shape of an Ice Cube Affects Rate of Melting
11. The Heat Capacities of Zinc and Copper
13. Does Shape Affect a Ball's Energy?

HOME

2. Graphing a Pendulum Swing
3. Metals in Electromagnets
4. Effectiveness of Plastic Wrap in Preventing Evaporation
5. Which Fruits and Vegetables Make the Best Batteries?
6. Do All Carbonated Beverages Go Flat at the Same Rate?
8. The Relationship of Temperature to Viscosity
9. Homemade Galvanometer
10. Which Type of Food Contains the Most Energy?
12. How Does LED Brightness Vary With Current?

OUTDOORS

Our Findings

1. ACCURACY OF LABELING VITAMIN C IN ORANGE JUICE

Idea for class discussion: Find out how many students have a glass of orange juice every day. Ask them to suggest some of the health benefits of orange juice.

Notes to the teacher: To prepare a 1 percent starch solution, add 0.5 grams (g) soluble starch to 50 milliliter (ml) of distilled water heated to near-boiling. Mix well and cool before using.

Analysis

1. Answers will vary depending on the brands chosen.

2. Student graphs should include four types of orange juice along the X-axis and the vitamin C content along the Y-axis. The vitamin C content of each type of juice should be represented by a bar of appropriate height.

3. Answers will vary based on experimental results.

4. Student graphs should include the four types of orange juice along the X-axis and the amount of iodine used along the Y-axis. The amount of iodine used in the titration for each type of juice should be represented by a bar of appropriate height.

5. Answers will vary. Students should compare the amount of vitamin C listed for each brand of juice to the amount of iodine required in the titration.

6. Answers will vary. Vitamin C is very reactive and will break down easily during shipping and time on the shelf at the grocery store. The amount of vitamin C can be impacted by the exposure to light, high temperatures, or exposure to air.

7. Answers will vary. Some sources of error include: over-shooting the titration, which causes the solution to turn darker than it should be at the endpoint; improper reading of the iodine levels in the burette; and inaccuracies in the measurement of orange juice that was added to the flask before testing.

2. GRAPHING A PENDULUM SWING

Idea for class discussion: Show the class a picture of a grandfather clock and point out the pendulum. Ask for ideas as to how the pendulum runs the clock. Revisit student ideas after the experiment.

Analysis

1. Answers will vary. Student answers may be similar to the following: "I predict that a longer pendulum will swing for a longer period of time and a shorter pendulum will swing for a shorter period of time."

2. Forces acting on the pendulum include gravity and friction (air resistance).

3. The friction caused by the molecules in the air, otherwise known as air resistance, causes the pendulum to slow to a stop.

4. Graphs will vary. The length of the pendulum should be on the X-axis and the period of the pendulum swing should be on the Y-axis. The length and period for each trial should be placed on the graph as a dot, and the lines should be connected to form a graph similar to the sample graph.

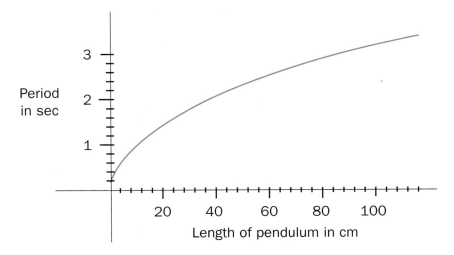

Sample answer to Analysis question 4

5. As the string length increases, the period increases. This is because a pendulum can swing a greater distance if the bob is attached to a longer string.

6. Answers will vary. Students might hypothesize that the mass of the bob increases or decreases the swing of the pendulum (but it does not).

7. Answers will vary based on experimental results.

3. METALS IN ELECTROMAGNETS

Idea for class discussion: On the board or overhead projector, draw a diagram of a wire surrounded by concentric circles. Explain that the circles represent the magnetic field produced when current flows through the wire. Ask students to suggest some ways to use this magnetic field.

Analysis

1. Answers will vary depending on student procedures. Some suggestions include making sure all nails are the same size, wrapping the wire around each different nail the same number of times, and using a new battery for each trial.

2. Answers may vary depending on student procedures, but the strength of their electromagnet could most easily be predicted by comparing the number of staples that could be picked up by each electromagnet.

3. strongest, iron; weakest, aluminum

4. Answers will vary. The magnetism of a piece of metal depends on the presence of domains. A domain is an area within a piece of metal in which electron spins are aligned. Each domain acts as a small magnet, and when domains are aligned, they create a strong magnetic field.

5. Since the metal used in this experiment does not act as a bar magnet, where all electrons are aligned, an electrical current must flow through the metal for there to be a net movement of electrons that creates a magnetic current.

4. EFFECTIVENESS OF PLASTIC WRAP IN PREVENTING EVAPORATION

Idea for class discussion: Show students a roll of plastic wrap and ask them to explain why consumers buy this type of product. Ask for details about the characteristics of this product that make it useful.

Analysis

1. Answers will vary. Students should provide a description of the physical characteristics of each brand of plastic wrap and compare characteristics such as appearance, texture, and strength.

2. Answers will vary. Students will choose the brand of plastic wrap they believe will prevent the most evaporation and one they believe will let the most water through. They should provide justification for their answer. For example, they might say that Glad™ wrap will prevent evaporation the best because it is the thickest and feels strongest.

3. Graphs will vary. Student graphs should be neatly drawn bar graphs comparing the three brands of plastic wrap. The plastic wrap brands should be labeled along the X-axis and the amount of water evaporated on the Y-axis.

4. Answers will vary. Students should identify the brand of plastic wrap that allowed the least amount of water evaporation.

5. Answers will vary. Students should compare their answer from question 4 with their prediction from question 2 and explain why their prediction did or did not agree with the results of the experiment.

6. Answers will vary. Students might describe some of the different uses of plastic wraps (such as protecting food from contamination, reducing water loss in food, storing food) and correlate the types of wrap to the specific uses.

5. WHICH FRUITS AND VEGETABLES MAKE THE BEST BATTERIES?

Idea for class discussion: Ask students to make a list of 10 devices that require batteries. Point out that batteries provide us with a portable source of electrical current.

Analysis

1. Answers will vary. Students should state which fruits or vegetables they chose to use as batteries and justify why they did so.

2. Answers will vary. Student hypothesis should include a prediction about which battery will produce the most electric current and an explanation of why they believe that will be so.

3. The copper serves as the cathode because it is less electronegative than zinc, and therefore it gives up electrons more easily. Zinc serves as the negative anode because it attracts electron more strongly than copper does.

4. If two of the same types of metal were used as electrodes, both substances would "pull" or "push" electrons with the same amount of force, and the electrical currents would cancel each other out.

5. Answers will vary. An acidic fruit, such as a lemon, will most likely produce the best battery. A very weak electrolyte will produce the worst battery. Student answers will depend on the fruits or vegetables chosen.

6. Strong electrolytes produce the best batteries. For instance, lemons make good batteries because they are highly acidic and have a large number of ions that will transfer electrons from the solution to the electrodes inserted into the fruit. Fruits and vegetables that are more neutral contain fewer ions and therefore do not conduct electrons effectively.

6. DO ALL CARBONATED BEVERAGES GO FLAT AT THE SAME RATE?

Idea for class discussion: Ask students to name their favorite carbonated drinks. Find out what the students know about the source of bubbles in carbonated drinks.

Analysis

1. Answers will vary depending on the types of soft drinks chosen. Students should describe the brand, flavor, and characteristics of each type of carbonated beverage chosen.

2. Answers will vary depending on student procedures. Possible answers include maintaining constant temperatures for all soft drinks, using the same size bottles, and the same brand of balloons.

3. Answers will vary, but possible answers include sealing each balloon tightly around the neck of each bottle and opening the caps inside the balloon so that no carbon dioxide escapes.

4. Graphs will vary. Student graphs should be labeled and include the five types of beverages across the X-axis and the amount of carbon dioxide released on the Y-axis.

5. Answers will vary depending on the beverages chosen and the experimental results.

6. Answers will vary. Possible answers include temperature, agitation (shaking or stirring), and amount of carbon dioxide originally in the beverage.

7. No. Generally seltzer and drinks with artificial sweeteners contain more carbon dioxide than soft drinks with sugar. Therefore, clear carbonated beverages and drinks with artificial sweeteners most likely released more carbon dioxide. Students know the relative amounts of carbon dioxide gas from each beverage because of the results of their own experiments.

7. THE SHAPE OF AN ICE CUBE AFFECTS RATE OF MELTING

Idea for class discussion: Ask two or three students to sketch the shape of "ice cubes" on the board. Shapes might include true cubes, cylinders, and crushed particles. Discuss the reasons for making cubes in different shapes.

Analysis

1. Answers will vary. Students should describe the six different shapes that were chosen for their ice molds.

2. Answers will vary. Students should choose the ice cube shape they believe will melt the fastest and the one that will melt the slowest. Students should justify their answers.

3. Answers will vary based on shapes chosen and experimental results.

4. Graphs will vary. Student graphs should be labeled and include a bar that represents each shape of ice cube and the time that it took for that shape to melt completely.

5. Answers will vary. Possible factors include a thin shape, several projections or intricate patterns, or an increased surface area.

6. The same volume should be used for each sample so that the shape will be the only experimental factor. All other variables should be kept constant.

7. A spherical shaped ice cube would have the lowest surface-area-to-volume ratio and would therefore melt the slowest.

8. Answers will vary. Possible sources of error include spilling water, not being able to determine when the ice had melted completely, and touching the ice cubes as they were melting.

8. THE RELATIONSHIP OF TEMPERATURE TO VISCOSITY

Idea for class discussion: Display several different types of lubricating oils and discuss some of their uses. Ask students why there are so many different types.

Notes to the teacher: Suggested motor oils are 5W-20, 10W-30, and 20W-50.

Analysis

1. Answers will vary depending on motor oil types chosen. Variable-

viscosity motor oils have two numbers listed in their rating. The first tells the winter viscosity rating and the second tells the rating at high temperatures. Therefore, the oil with the highest numbers listed as the first rating will have the highest viscosity at low temperatures. One type of high-viscosity oil is 20W-50.

2. Answers will vary based on experimental results. Students should tell whether their results agreed with the expected outcome and provide an explanation describing why that was so.

3. Graphs will vary based on student results. All parts of the graph should be labeled and they should include three different colored lines, each connecting two points. Each of the points should depict the amount of time it took for the marble to fall at each temperature.

4. The variable-viscosity motor oil will thin slightly as it is heated, but not as much as motor oil with only one temperature rating.

5. Low viscosity is important in cold temperatures because it allows the engine parts to move without hindrance from a thick motor oil. High-viscosity oils are thicker and protect an engine better at higher temperatures; therefore, they are recommended for hot weather.

6. Answers will vary based on experimental results and the samples chosen. The motor oil with a higher viscosity rating would be best to use in warm temperatures, while the oil with the lower reading will be better suited for cold weather.

9. HOMEMADE GALVANOMETER

Idea for class discussion: Ask students to suggest some uses of a galvanometer. They might suggest using it to measure electric current flowing through a wire, an electrical socket, or a battery.

Analysis

1. Answers will vary. The compass needle moves because it points in the direction of a positive charge (such as magnetic north), and when the battery is connected, it points toward the positive charge, indicating the direction of the flow of electrons.

2. Answers will vary. A compass will point toward magnetic north because collectively, electrons flow from the magnetic south pole toward magnetic north. The compass will point in the direction of electron flow

3. Answers will vary based on experimental results. The needle will move toward the direction of electron flow, from the negative end of the battery to the positive end.

4. After the battery was removed, the compass needle pointed toward magnetic north. In the absence of a direct electrical flow, the needle picked up on Earth's magnetic field once again.

5. The galvanometer needle moved, indicating the strength and direction of electron flow.

6. Answers will vary, but may include the following: Both meters used needles and had wires to connect to the battery. The direction of needle movement changed when the wires were switched for each galvanometer. The actual galvanometer tells the strength of the electric current, while the student-constructed one does not. The compass needle spins while connected, while the galvanometer needle moves from the central point and rests on a particular number.

7. Answers will vary. Possible answers include: the galvanometer could be used to measure the power coming from an electromagnet, the amount of current flowing in any closed system.

10. WHICH TYPE OF FOOD CONTAINS THE MOST ENERGY?

Ideas for class discussion: Distribute the wrappers for several snack food and have students note the calories per serving. Ask students to offer their own definition of "calorie." Revisit their definitions after the experiment.

Analysis

1. Answers will vary depending on the foods chosen. Students should describe the food items that they are choosing to test and predict which one will contain the most energy.

2. Answers will vary. Students should list all four foods and the calories contained in a serving of each, according to the nutrition label.

3. Answers will vary. Students should show calculations and record their answers on Data Table 2.

4. Answers will vary. Students should show calculations and record their answers on Data Table 2.

5. Answers will vary. Students should plug the data from the appropriate columns of Data Table 2 into the equation $Q = m \times C \times \Delta T$. They should show all work and record their calculated Q values on Data Table 2.

6. Answers will vary. Students should divide their answers from question 5 by the mass of each food sample that was burned to calculate the calories contained in each gram of each type of food.

7. Answers will vary. Students should compare their results from question 6 with the food label results from question 2.

8. Answers will vary. Some sources of error include: Heat is lost to the environment and cannot be measured in the experiment. Some portions of the food sample could have been lost in the burning process and could not be weighed after the experiment. The fire could have gone out prematurely; causing incomplete combustion of the food.

11. THE HEAT CAPACITIES OF ZINC AND COPPER

Idea for class discussion: Ask students to offer some ideas about why pots and pans are made of metals. Revisit their ideas after the experiment.

Notes to the teacher: The specific heat of copper is 0.385. The specific heat of zinc is 0.3884.

Analysis

1. Answers will vary based on experiment results. The temperature of the water should increase by only a few degrees Celsius (°C).

2. Answers will vary based on experiment results. The temperature change should be negative, as the metal will cool by about 65 to 75°C.

3. Answers will vary based on experiment results. Students should use the equation $C_{p2} = m_1 C_{p1} \Delta T_1 / -(m_2 \Delta T_2)$. The value for m_1 is the mass of water, m_2 is the mass of the metal, ΔT_1 is the temperature change from sample 1, ΔT_2 is the temperature change from sample 2, and C_{p1} is 4.184 J/g°C (the specific heat of water).

4. Answers will vary based on experiment results. The specific heat of copper is as follows: 0.385 J/g°C. % error = (|actual value − experimental value| / actual value) × 100%.

5. Answers will vary based on experiment results. The temperature of the water should increase by only a few degrees Celsius.

6. Answers will vary based on experiment results. The temperature change should be negative, as the metal will cool by about 65 to 75°C.

7. Answers will vary based on experiment results. Students should use the equation $C_{p2} = m_1 C_{p1} \Delta T_1 / - (m_2 \Delta T_2)$. The value for m_1 is the mass of water, m_2 is the mass of the metal, ΔT_1 is the temperature change from question 5, ΔT_2 is the temperature change from question 6, and C_{p1} is 4.184 $J/g°C$ (the specific heat of water).

8. Answers will vary based on experiment results. The specific heat of zinc is 0.3884 $J/g°C$. % error = (|actual value – experimental value| / actual value) × 100%.

9. Answers will vary. Sources of error include inaccurate temperature or mass measurements, heat loss from the calorimeter, and heat loss from the metal as it was transferred from the boiling water to the calorimeter.

12. HOW DOES LED BRIGHTNESS VARY WITH CURRENT?

Idea for class discussion: Show students a string of LED Christmas lights and a similar string of incandescent lights. Ask them to point out some of the obvious differences in the two. Point out the fact that LEDs use less electricity than other types of bulbs.

Analysis

1. Yes; current will not flow within a circuit unless there is a connection between the positive and negative ends of a battery so that they flow of electrons can be complete.

2. A resistor slows the flow of charged particles within a circuit so that the amount of current can be controlled.

3. Answers may vary. Suggested answer: If no resistor were used it could drain the battery or cause damage to the LED.

4. Student graphs will vary. Graphs should include five points depicting the light intensity produced from each of the circuits with varying resistor strength. The light intensity should decrease as resistor strength increases.

5. As resistor strength decreases, light intensity increases.

6. Ohm's law states that current, resistance, and voltage are related. Therefore, as resistance increases, the current decreases proportionally. This should be indicated in the brightness of the LED lights.

7. Answers will vary based on the resistance ratings chosen. Using the equation, $I = E/R$, students should plug 4.5 volts in as E and the resistance ratings in as R, and calculate I for each of the trials.

13. DOES SHAPE AFFECT A BALL'S ENERGY?

Idea for class discussion: Ask students why most balls are round? Elicit from students the idea that shape is related to a ball's bounce.

Analysis:

1. Student sketches of the balls they created will vary.

2. Answers will vary based on the shapes created. Spherical shapes bounce the highest, while flattened shapes will bounce the least.

3. Student graphs will vary. Bar graphs should contain four bars depicting the height of the bounce for each of the shapes created. Height in centimeters should be labeled on the Y-axis. All parts of the graph should be labeled.

4. Answers will vary based on the shapes created. Rounded shapes will generally bounce the highest while shapes with flat edges tend to have the lowest bounce.

5. Answers will vary. Students should state whether or not their predictions were correct and justify their answers.

6. Conclusion statements will vary. Student conclusions should include a discussion of each ball, its shape, the height of its bounce, and an explaination of how shape influenced its bounce. Student answers should relate their findings to the kinetic and potential energy transfer that occurred when they bounced each ball.

14. WHICH MATERIALS ARE THE BEST SOUND INSULATORS?

Idea for class discussion: Ask students to imagine that they are working as designers on a construction project for the new music wing of a school. Explain that each of the practice rooms in the new wing must be built so sound does not travel from one room to the next. Ask for suggestions about how to do this.

Analysis

1. Answers will vary. Students should describe properties that they feel will make a good soundproofing material and justify their answer.

2. Answers will vary. Students should predict which material will allow more sound to pass through them.

3. Student hypotheses will vary. Students should choose the material that they think will soundproof the best and explain why they think so.

4. Answers will vary. Some answers may include playing the same song on the radio or MP3 player for each trial, using the same box for each trial, and measuring the distance from the box to where the listener stood. In a controlled experiment, only one variable can be tested.

5. Answer will vary based on experimental results.

6. Answer will vary based on experimental results.

7. Answers will vary. Students should state whether or not their results matched their predictions and provide an explanation if they did not.

15. MATERIALS THAT INTERFERE WITH MAGNETIC ENERGY

Idea for class discussion: Perform a demonstration by sprinkling some iron filings on a table top and using a magnet underneath the table to move the filings. Ask students to explain what is happening. Elicit the conclusion that the magnetic field travels through the table top.

Notes to the teacher: If you do not have samples of steel, iron, and copper, students can use cookware. Have students hold the side or the bottom of a piece of cookware between the magnet and the paper clip.

Analysis

1. Answers will vary. Students should describe how the paper clip was attracted to the magnet, how it pulled the paper clip from a distance and then attached to it.

2. Answers will vary. Students should predict which metal will produce the best magnetic field blocker and justify their answer.

3. Student graphs will vary. The bar graph should include 10 bars, one for each type of material used, and should compare the force used to

remove the paper clip from the magnet. All parts of the graph should be labeled.

4. Answers will vary based on student results. Most likely, the answer will be iron.

5. Answers will vary based on student results. Most likely, the answer will be paper.

6. Answers will vary; some possible answers include: magnetic, composed of metal, thick.

16. DOES THE DIAMETER OF A SPEAKING TUBE AFFECT VOLUME?

Idea for class discussion: Discuss the properties of sound waves with students. Ask them to explain how sound waves change when volume of the sound increases.

Analysis

1. Answers will vary, but should resemble the diagram below.

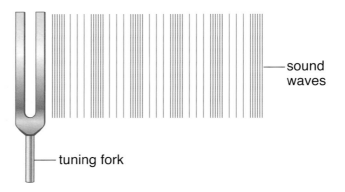

Sample answer to question 1.

2. Answers will vary. Drawings should show that a megaphone prevents sound waves from scattering from the source, directing them toward a target.

3. Answers will vary. As a sound waves moves suddenly from a narrow space to an open one, some of the wave is reflected back toward the source. A megaphone reduces the amount of sound that is reflected back by providing a gradual shift from the mouth to the air.

4. Student answers will vary. Students should predict which megaphone will produce the loudest sound and explain why.

5. Student graphs will vary. Graphs should contain points connected by lines with all parts of the graph labeled.

6. The sound is amplified more as the diameter increases. However, if the diameter increases too much (so that the megaphone is no longer tube-shaped), it will no longer amplify the sound because the megaphone will no longer focus the sound in one direction.

7. Answers will vary. The cone shape focuses the sound so that all of the energy moves in one direction instead of in a circular pattern from the origin. The widened end enables the sound to resound and spread out once again so that the sound waves can be dispersed again in the direction in which they were focused.

17. COMPARING DENSITIES OF A SOLID, LIQUID, AND GAS

Idea for class discussion: Have students describe the three phases or states of matter. Ask them how the behavior of molecules in each phase differs.

Analysis

1. Solid. In solid materials, particles are very close together. In liquids and gases, particles are more widely spaced.

2. The volume of a regularly shaped solid can be found by multiplying length times width times height. In irregularly shaped solids, volume can be determined through water displacement.

3. The volume of a liquid can be found with a graduated cylinder.

4. wood; air

5. 2.70 grams per milliliter (g/ml)

6. Student answers will vary but should include ice, liquid water, and steam.

18. WHAT ARE THE BEST FRICTION-REDUCING LUBRICANTS?

Idea for class discussion: Ask students to give their own definitions of "friction." Ask them to suggest some ways to reduce friction.

Analysis

1. Answers will vary. Students should predict which lubricant will work best and which one will reduce the friction the least.

2. Answers will vary. Students should justify their answers based on their observations of the lubricant properties.

3. Graphs will vary based on experimental results. Each graph should include a bar representing the time for each trial and include a title and labels for each axis of the graph.

4. Answers will vary based on experiment results.

5. Answers will vary based on experiment results. Most likely, a thin, oily lubricant such as baby oil or mineral oil will have the best lubricating effects in these conditions.

6. There are a lot of different lubricants because they are designed to do different jobs. Different lubricants are used in varying situations. Lubricants are made from a variety of different compounds. Some lubricants may be more efficient at different temperatures or for different purposes. Some may also contain chemicals or additives that will work with certain surfaces, but be damaging to others.

19. ARROW MASS AND DEPTH OF PENETRATION

Idea for class discussion: Ask how many students have used a bow and arrow. Have one or two recount their personal experiences. If possible, show the students a short video clip of an archer shooting a bow such as the footage from 2009 Olympics at http://www.nbcolympics.com/archery/video/all/index.html. Alternately, share with the class two or three different arrow tips and ask why archers might use different tips.

Analysis

1. Student hypotheses will vary. Students should predict the effect that arrow mass will have on depth of penetration and explain their reasons for the predictions that they make.

2. Answers will vary. Possible answers include using the same arrow for each trial, shooting from the same distance, pulling the bow back the same distance each time, having the same body form for each trial, and aiming correctly.

3. Answers may vary based on experiment results, but it will most likely be the 125-grain arrow.

4. Answers will vary based on student hypothesis and experiment results. Students should explain why their hypothesis was incorrect if it was proven to be so.

5. Conclusion statements will vary, but they should include a thorough discussion of the relationship between arrow mass and depth of penetration and an explanation of why the experiment results turned out as they did.

6. Answers may vary. Possible answers include wind, improper form, bad aim, or measurement error.

20. VARIABLES THAT AFFECT SPEED

Idea for class discussion: Ask students to imagine a sled race in which two people are riding down a slope on identical sleds. One person weighs 300 pounds (136 kilograms) and the other one weighs 100 pounds (45.35 kilograms). Ask students who they think will win the race and why.

Notes to teacher: Younger students will require supervision if they choose to use hammer and nails.

Analysis

1. Student hypotheses will vary. They should choose the variable that they think will increase the speed of the ball most and explain why they think it will do so.

2. Answers will vary based on student procedures. Students should explain their control factors within the experiment. For example, they should use the same ball and same track length if they are testing the angle of the ramp as a variable. If the mass of the ball is being tested, the track length and height should remain constant.

3. It is important to change only one variable in a controlled experiment so that you can prove that the variable being tested was the only thing that could have affected the outcome of the experiment.

4. Answers will vary. Some sources of error may include problems with ramp construction, varying the release point, and varying the force with which the ball was pushed.

5. Answers will vary. Students may suggest ramp designs that provide better data for analysis.

Glossary

acceleration   rate at which velocity changes

ammeter   instrument that measures the flow in an electrical current

anode   the negative terminal of a battery

antioxidants   molecules that slow or stop other molecules from chemically reacting with oxygen

archery   sport in which a bow is used to shoot arrows

biodegradable   able to be decomposed by bacteria or fungi into simpler substance

Bose-Einstein condensate   a gaseous state of matter, formed near absolute zero, in which all atoms behave as one super atom

buoyant force   upward force on an object that enables it to float or rise toward the surface of a liquid

calorie   the amount of heat needed to raise the temperature of a kilogram (kg) of water 1 degree Celsius (°C).

calorimeter   device used to measure the amount of heat released by an object

calorimetry   science of measuring heat released in chemical reactions

cardinal directions   the four main points on a compass: north, south, east, and west

cathode   the positive terminal on a battery

cellulose   strong, rigid complex carbohydrate that provides support and structure in plants

coefficient of friction   the ratio of the force needed for two surfaces to slide past each other; the lower the ratio, the less the resistance due to friction

cofactor   substance that works with a chemical to carry out a chemical reaction

condense   change from a gas to a liquid or solid

current   flow of electricity through a circuit

density   mass of an object per unit volume

dipole   an object that has equal and opposite charges at its ends, or poles

domain   region within a magnet in which atoms are spinning in the same direction

echo   a repeating sound caused by the reflection of sound waves

electricity   the flow of electrons through a conductor

electrolyte   substance containing free ions that is able to conduct an electrical current

electromagnet   temporary magnet produced when electricity flows through a wire that is wrapped around a metal core

electromagnetic field   field of force that results from passing an electrical current through a wire

endothermic reaction   type of chemical reaction that requires heat

entropy   the amount of energy in a system that is no longer available to do work

evaporate   change from a liquid to a gas

exothermic reaction   type of chemical reaction that releases heat

force   a push or pull that can cause an object with mass to accelerate

Foucault's pendulum   a pendulum that is free to move in any direction and that demonstrates the Earth's rotation

frequency   number of waves that pass a point in 1 second

friction   force that resists the motion of two objects against each other

galvanometer   type of ammeter that is used to measure small electrical currents

grain   measurement of weight in arrow tips; 7,000 grains are equivalent to 1 pound

greenhouse gases   atmospheric gases, primarily water vapor, methane, carbon dioxide, and ozone, that trap the Sun's heat near Earth's surface

heat capacity   amount of heat required to raise the temperature of 1 gram (g) of a substance 1 degree Celsius (°C)

inclined plane   simple machine that reduces effort force by increasing distance

ion   atom or molecule that is positively or negatively charged

joule   unit for measuring energy; 1 joule of energy is expended to move 1 amp of current through 1 ohm of resistance

kinetic energy   energy that an object possesses due to motion

light-emitting diode   type of semiconductor that emits light when a current travels through it

longitudinal wave   wave that vibrates parallel to its direction of motion

lubricant   substance that reduces friction between two objects

matter   anything that has mass and takes up space

megaphone   funnel-shaped device that is used to increased the volume of a person's voice

mu metal   an alloy of nickel and iron that is not permeable to a magnetic field, so can be used to screen magnetic fields

net force   combination of all the forces acting on an object

neutralization   chemical reaction in which an acid and base react to form water and a salt

n region   area of a semiconducting chip that is primarily positively charged

ohm   unit of resistance of the flow of electricity through a conductor

Ohm's law   law stating that 1 volt of electrical current is needed to push 1 amp of current through 1 ohm of resistance

oxidation-reduction reaction   chemical reaction in which the oxidized substance gives up electrons and the reduced substance gains electrons

oxidize   to lose electrons to another substance, usually oxygen, through a chemical reaction resulting in the break down of a complex compound

pendulum   a mass attached to a pivot from which it can swing freely

period   the time required to finish one cycle of a repeating event

photon   a bundle of energy carried by light

physical change   type of change that does not produce a new substance, such as a change in phase

plasma   a state of matter in which a superheated material loses its electrons, resulting in an ionized gas

polyvinyl chloride   a synthetic polymer that can be used to make a number of products, including plastic wrap, cable covers, and pipes

polyvinylidene chloride a synthetic polymer that is often used to make a thin, transparent film

potential energy energy of an object resulting from its position

precipitation any form of water that falls to the Earth

p region area of a semiconducting chip that is negatively charged

projectile an object projected into a gravitational field by the exertion of a force

reduce to add electrons to an object during a chemical reaction

resistor material that reduces the flow of electrical current through a circuit

scurvy condition caused by lack of vitamin C that results in weakness, bleeding under the skin, and spongy gums

speed distance traveled per unit time

surface area the amount of exterior surface of an object

thermodynamics branch of physics that studies the conversion of heat to other forms of energy

titration method of finding the concentration of an acid or based by neutralizing it

vacuum space that is empty of matter

viscosity measure of the resistance of a liquid to flow

vitamin C ascorbic acid, an essential, water-soluble vitamin that has many functions in the body

voltage unit used to measure the potential or pressure of an electric current

water cycle natural cycle of water through the environment which includes evaporation, condensation, and precipitation

Internet Resources

The World Wide Web is an invaluable source of information for students, teachers, and parents. The following list is intended to help you get started exploring educational sites that relate to the book. This list is just a sample of the Web material that is available to you. All of these sites were accessible as of March 2009.

Educational Resources

American Chemical Society. "Periodic Table of the Elements." Available online. URL: http://acswebcontent.acs.org/games/pt.html. Accessed March 5, 2009. This interactive Web page is devoted to the Periodic Table and offers up-to-date information on its elements and electron configurations.

"Carbonated Drinks." Available online. URL: http://u-fizz.com/files/HowCarbonationWorks.ppt. Accessed March 13, 2009. This PowerPoint presentation on carbonation explains the basic concepts of gas solubility using simple language and great visuals.

Chem 1 Virtual Chemistry Textbook. "Getting Started," March 26, 2007. Available online. URL: http://www.chem1.com/acad/webtext/pre/index.html. Accessed March 13, 2009. This Web page provides information on several topics of basic chemistry, including properties of matter, energy, and units of measurement.

EnergyPortal.EU. "What Is a Battery and How Does It Work?" July 4, 2006. Available online. URL: http://www.energyportal.eu/reviews/green-energy/34-what-is-a-battery-and-how-does-it-work.html. Accessed March 13, 2009. This Web page lists the parts of a battery and explains how rechargeable batteries work.

Greenslade, Thomas J. "Electricity," *Instruments of Natural Philosophy*. Available online. URL: http://physics.kenyon.edu/EarlyApparatus/Titlepage/Electricity.html. Accessed March 13, 2009. Greenslade shares his photographs of early devices used in the study of electricity, including electromagnets from the 17th century.

Henderson, Tom. "The Physics Classroom Tutorial," 2007. Available online. URL: http://www.glenbrook.k12.il.us/GBSSCI/PHYS/CLASS/sound/soundtoc.html. Henderson's Web site offers information on several topics in physics, including sound waves.

Higdon, Jane. "Vitamin C," Linus Pauling Institute, October 17, 2008. Available online. URL: http://lpi.oregonstate.edu/infocenter/vitamins/vitaminC/. Accessed March 13, 2009. Higdon discusses the many roles of vitamin C in the body, including its antioxidant properties, on this Web site.

Kurtus, Ron. "Pendulum Exhibits Periodic Motion," School of Champions, November 13, 2006. Available online. URL: http://www.school-for-champions.com/science/pendulum.htm. Accessed March 13, 2009. On this Web page, Kurtus discusses the physics of pendulums, including frequency and period.

Rader's Chem4Kids.com. 2007. Available online. URL: http://www.chem4kids.com/index.html. Accessed March 13, 2009. Chem4Kids describes several chemical principles using simple language and color figures.

ScienceDaily. "Almost Frictionless Gears With Liquid Crystal Lubricants," November 11, 2008. Available online. URL: http://www.sciencedaily.com/releases/2008/11/081110112140.htm. Accessed March 13, 2009. This article explains how liquid crystals are being tested for their lubricating properties.

U.S. Food and Drug Administration. Available online. URL: http://www.fda.gov/. Accessed July 1, 2009. The FDA Web page provides information on food ingredients and packaging as well as labeling, safety, and nutrition.

Periodic Table of Elements

Key:
- 1 — atomic number
- H — symbol
- 1.008 — atomic weight

Numbers in parentheses are the atomic mass numbers of radioactive isotopes.

1	2	3	4	5	6	7	8	9	10	11	12	13	14	15	16	17	18
1 H 1.008																	2 He 4.003
3 Li 6.941	4 Be 9.012											5 B 10.81	6 C 12.01	7 N 14.01	8 O 16.00	9 F 19.00	10 Ne 20.18
11 Na 22.99	12 Mg 24.31											13 Al 26.98	14 Si 28.09	15 P 30.97	16 S 32.07	17 Cl 35.45	18 Ar 39.95
19 K 39.10	20 Ca 40.08	21 Sc 44.96	22 Ti 47.88	23 V 50.94	24 Cr 52.0	25 Mn 54.94	26 Fe 55.85	27 Co 58.93	28 Ni 58.69	29 Cu 63.55	30 Zn 65.39	31 Ga 69.72	32 Ge 72.59	33 As 74.92	34 Se 78.96	35 Br 79.90	36 Kr 83.80
37 Rb 85.47	38 Sr 87.62	39 Y 88.91	40 Zr 91.22	41 Nb 92.91	42 Mo 95.94	43 Tc (98)	44 Ru 101.1	45 Rh 102.9	46 Pd 106.4	47 Ag 107.9	48 Cd 112.4	49 In 114.8	50 Sn 118.7	51 Sb 121.8	52 Te 127.6	53 I 126.9	54 Xe 131.3
55 Cs 132.9	56 Ba 137.3	57-71*	72 Hf 178.5	73 Ta 180.9	74 W 183.9	75 Re 186.2	76 Os 190.2	77 Ir 192.2	78 Pt 195.1	79 Au 197.0	80 Hg 200.6	81 Tl 204.4	82 Pb 207.2	83 Bi 209.0	84 Po (210)	85 At (210)	86 Rn (222)
87 Fr (223)	88 Ra (226)	89-103‡	104 Rf (261)	105 Db (262)	106 Sg (263)	107 Bh (262)	108 Hs (265)	109 Mt (266)	110 Ds (271)	111 Rg (272)	112 Uub (285)		114 Uuq (285)		116 Uuh (292)		118 Uuo (?)

*lanthanide series

57 La 138.9	58 Ce 140.1	59 Pr 140.9	60 Nd 144.2	61 Pm (145)	62 Sm 150.4	63 Eu 152.0	64 Gd 157.3	65 Tb 158.9	66 Dy 162.5	67 Ho 164.9	68 Er 167.3	69 Tm 168.9	70 Yb 173.0	71 Lu 175.0

‡actinide series

89 Ac (227)	90 Th 232.0	91 Pa 231.0	92 U 238.0	93 Np (237)	94 Pu (244)	95 Am (243)	96 Cm (247)	97 Bk (247)	98 Cf (251)	99 Es (252)	100 Fm (257)	101 Md (258)	102 No (259)	103 Lr (260)

Index